D0671266

Paul Duncan

The Pocket Essential

STANLEY KUBRICK

---

www.pocketessentials.com

First published in Great Britain 1999 - this revised and updated edition published 2002 by Pocket Essentials, 18 Coleswood Road, Harpenden, Herts, AL5 1EQ

Distributed in the USA by Trafalgar Square Publishing, PO Box 257, Howe Hill Road, North Pomfret, Vermont 05053

A CIP catalogue record for this book is available from the British Library.

ISBN 1-903047-01-3

4 6 8 10 9 7 5 3

Book typeset by Pdunk
Printed and bound by Cox & Wyman

For Claude and Josef

Acknowledgements

My thanks to the resourceful John Ashbrook for his help in my research. As ever, I thank Claude and Josef for attempting to keep me sane - better luck next time.

CONTENTS

Stanley Kubrick: Eyewitness

I was walking around a Robert Capa exhibition recently. Capa was a war photographer who made his name with stunning pictures of the Spanish Civil War and became one of the founders of the world-famous Magnum photo agency. His name came back into circulation when his blurred pictures of the D-Day landing on Omaha Beach were the inspiration for the filming style of Steven Spielberg's *Saving Private Ryan*. The reason I mention Capa is that as I stood in front of the photos - whether it was Matisse bent at 90 degrees drawing giant sketches with a long stick, or Chinese children frantically involved in a snowball fight amidst the Japanese invasion, or the grieving widows of Italian fighters, or American GIs talking to English kids - they were so perfectly framed and realised, that I was there, and it was happening to me. They were no longer images - they were experiences.

In our daily lives, we are constantly surrounded by diverse images. Where once the written word was king, now images have taken their place. The spoken word is subservient to a series of moving images. But the power of the image has been diluted from overuse. Here, then, is Stanley Kubrick, who started as a photographer for *Look* magazine (straight from school, aged 17), who told stories through his images, who meticulously collected images for his movies, so that when that image moves, it moves from one perfectly framed and realised image to another.

It was always difficult to predict the subjects of Kubrick's films. He straddled genres like a colossus.

Kubrick directed four anti-war films *Fear And Desire* (1953), *Paths Of Glory* (1957), *Dr Strangelove* (1964) and *Full Metal Jacket* (1987). *Fear And Desire*, which Kubrick produced, edited and served as director of photography, was made for only $10,000 and is little-seen today, mainly because there is only one known print in existence and it's in private hands. Supposed to be badly made and pretentious, it's probably just as well. *Paths Of Glory*, starring Kirk Douglas, is gut-wrenching - based on a true incident, it shows how soldiers are unjustly killed by their superiors because of ambition, pride and snobbery. Many regard this as Kubrick's best. *Dr Strangelove* is a unique depiction of the madness of war. It is a cold war black comedy that everybody took seriously.

Full Metal Jacket shows soldiers being stripped of their humanity and then being put in a situation where they have to kill. Some can do it, some can't.

Early on, there were a couple of crime films: *Killer's Kiss* (1955) and *The Killing* (1956). The former has some bad acting bolstered with some great directing. The latter was Kubrick's breakthrough movie. Famed for its racetrack robbery depicted in fractured time, people credit Kubrick with the technique when, in fact, it is in Lionel White's source novel *Clean Break*. It is a great crime movie about the fallibility of man.

After some writing on *One-Eyed Jacks*, eventually directed by Marlon Brando, Kubrick took over from Anthony Mann on *Spartacus* (1960). At the time it was the most expensive film ever made and won Kubrick many admirers because of the stunning photography perfectly combined with intimate acting. I rushed to my local multiplex when it was re-released and was knocked out seeing the movie on the big screen - pity I was the only one there. For all the plaudits, it was Kubrick's worst film experience and he decided never to do a Hollywood film again. Kubrick's roots were as an independent film-maker, and he continued with that attitude throughout the rest of his career.

And then, there were some decidedly different approaches to cinema. *2001: A Space Odyssey* (1968) is visual poetry. It is full of optimism, showing how man has used tools to extend his physical reach, but needs a little help to advance onto the next stage of evolution. *A Clockwork Orange* (1971) uses a futuristic setting to explore attitudes to violence, and who takes responsibility for it. *The Shining* (1980) uses the horror genre to explore the creative urge subsumed by sloth and other pleasures of the flesh.

Most of Kubrick's films show his characters in relation to, and their interaction with, their environment. It is this 'coldness' to people which has been a sticking point with some critics. (Some people even make the mistake of assuming that because Kubrick shows 'cold' people, then Kubrick was also emotionless, which is a ridiculous notion. If you follow that argument, then Martin Scorsese, Quentin Tarantino, Harvey Keitel and Robert De Niro must be killing people all the time.) Kubrick examined human emotions closely in the love stories of *Lolita* (1962), *Barry Lyndon* (1975) and *Eyes Wide Shut*.(1999).

We watch and listen to Kubrick's films. The stories end but the over-all meaning is ambiguous. We have to think about the films, interpret them through our own value systems and experience and then draw conclusions. This is what works of art do - they make you think about yourself and others. Interestingly, you can return to Kubrick's work many years later with different value systems, having gained more experience, and draw other conclusions.

What message does Kubrick have for us? Man is in constant conflict with his environment. This can be the social or political environment, or his fellow men. More often than not, the conflict is within himself. In *Killer's Kiss, Lolita* and *Eyes Wide Shut* the characters are looking for love. In *The Killing* and *Barry Lyndon* the characters want money - as a substitute for love? In *Paths Of Glory, Spartacus* and *A Clockwork Orange* physical and mental freedom is sought but society is too rigid to allow these. In *Dr Strangelove, 2001, The Shining* and *Full Metal Jacket* the characters dislike their present environment and want to change it, only the environment changes them. In the case of Bowman in *2001*, he physically changes into the Starchild.

Kubrick used very few stylistic devices. He simply picked the best place for the camera and rolled the film. Occasionally, he would indulge himself with visual ideas. Everybody remembers the gateway scene in *2001*, when Bowman travels through space visiting strange and wondrous places. He travels through a corridor of light. That movement through corridors occurs throughout Kubrick's film-making career, whether it is Colonel Dax walking through the trenches of *Paths Of Glory*, or Danny running through the maze at the end of *The Shining*.

Often, the corridor shot is combined with a reverse-tracking shot. This is when the camera is in front of a moving character, looking back at the character. Usually, the camera is low, looking up at the character, to give them more power. Kubrick used reverse tracking on his very first film, the documentary short called *The Day Of The Fight* (1950), when the twins Walter and Victor Cartier are walking down the street.

Ever since he was young, Kubrick liked the feel of a camera in his hand, and just because he was the director it didn't mean that he excluded himself from actually holding the camera. Like a kid with a new toy, Kubrick was always picking up a small movie camera and running around filming the actors doing their thing. This sometimes gave the footage a documentary edge. Kubrick often used a hand-held camera when his characters fought, like the bare-knuckle fight in *Barry Lyndon* or the rape scene in *A Clockwork Orange*, to give a sense of immediacy.

To cut down on the number of lights to think about (films are often made with many lights on a sound stage), Kubrick insisted that only source light be used. In *The Killing*, characters are assembled in a circle around a lamp, or under a light. In *Dr Strangelove*, Merkin Muffley and the Chiefs of Staff sit under an enormous circular light in the War Room.

It has often been claimed that Kubrick's interest in the game of chess led him to remain calm in a crisis and apply a methodical approach to the job in hand. Certainly there was often order and symmetry in the visual compositions. When the soldiers parade in *Paths Of Glory*, *Spartacus*, *Barry Lyndon* and *Full Metal Jacket*, they are in formation, as are the shots that frame them. There are many symmetrical shots in his movies.

Kubrick liked voice-overs. Perhaps this came from his documentary roots. *The Killing* has an authoritative narrator giving the facts throughout the movie, whilst *Barry Lyndon* has a witty and ironic voice commenting on the proceedings. Sometimes the central character speaks for himself: Davy in *Killer's Kiss*; Humbert in *Lolita*; Alex in *A Clockwork Orange*; and Joker in *Full Metal Jacket*.

It is interesting watching the films again, in sequence, because certain ideas, patterns and images emerge. Perhaps Kubrick's love of boxing influenced him to feature hand-to-hand fights - violence exploding onto the screen with a hand-held camera. Many of his characters are nice to animals - Alex loves his pet snake Basil more than he loves any human being. A lot of intense staring goes on in Kubrick films - it is a moment when time stops still and the inner demons and torment of the character are revealed.

Irony plays a large part in Kubrick's films. For example, when the characters play games (where people learn to deal with conflict), or wear masks/disguises (to reveal their true nature). *Barry Lyndon* opens with a game of cards where Nora flirts with Redmond - Redmond does not know how to play the game (of love), but spends the rest of the film gambling and winning (money, not love). In *A Clockwork Orange*, Alex and his droogs raid a house wearing masks that depict them to be monsters, which they are.

People and buildings from the late 18th and early 19th century proliferate in Kubrick's work (the room at the end of *2001*, the château in *Paths Of Glory*, the crowd watching Alex cavorting at the end of *A*

Clockwork Orange) and of course the music (do the words Strauss and *The Blue Danube* mean anything to you?). For many years Kubrick dreamed of directing a film about Napoleon - I suspect this period in history interested him because of his parents' roots in old Viennese culture.

Kubrick was not rooted in the past - he learnt from it. Kubrick was so modern he was ahead of his time. He invented or encouraged ways of filming now used as standard: taking Polaroids to get lighting/colour levels; video cameras to playback scenes before the film is exposed; the lenses he developed for *Barry Lyndon* were sought after by other cinematographers; he pushed Steadicam inventor Garrett Brown and used the technology in *The Shining*. Kubrick invented little gadgets and devices for his own personal use, and gave his family the very latest gadgets as Christmas presents. On more than one occasion, Kubrick would tell a lens or camera maker to do so-and-so to such-and-such and he would be told it was impossible. Then they would carry out Kubrick's instructions and find him to be correct - Kubrick had already worked out the science and mathematics. His intelligence and creativity were always backed up with research and facts.

Technology is often used as a subject within his films. In *2001*, tools are the subject - the HAL 9000 computer goes wrong, just as the methods for releasing nuclear devices go wrong in *Dr Strangelove*. Kubrick points out that the people and systems which govern our lives are wrong: General Mireau is willing to sacrifice thousands of men just so he can get a promotion in *Paths Of Glory*; everybody in *Lolita* is sexually promiscuous but the only one in love is Humbert the child abuser; the government portrayed as a nanny state in *A Clockwork Orange*; the unseen political figures create a situation in *Full Metal Jacket* where men become monsters.

Kubrick presented his ideas by arranging a triangle of relationships in each of his films - a central character and two choices. The conflict, drama and impetus of the film came from the decision-making process the central character undergoes. For example, in *Paths Of Glory* Kirk Douglas must decide whether to become a bureaucratic general or a slobbish soldier. Kubrick used the trial of the deserters to show us Douglas' thoughts on the matter - Douglas is repulsed by both options. In the end, Douglas decides he is his own man - he's a rebel without a cause, he is better than them all.

In *2001: A Space Odyssey*, perhaps Kubrick's most difficult film to analyse, the subject is man's evolution, and man is so concerned about his tools (the bone, the spacecraft, the computer) that he forgets his physical development. In a rare moment of optimism, Kubrick gives us the liberating experience of seeing man evolve beyond external tools. However, he does not give us any idea about the possible future emotional and spiritual development of man - if man uses his tools for killing, then he may also use his new body for killing.

In Kubrick's last film, *Eyes Wide Shut*, Dr Harford has to decide whether to remain faithful to his wife, or to revenge her infidelity with an imaginary lover by taking a lover of his own. In *Full Metal Jacket*, Joker must decide whether or not to kill the Vietnamese - he spends most of the movie trying to avoid the decision. In *A Clockwork Orange*, the theme is whether or not evil men like Alex should be allowed to have a choice at all.

Kubrick was labelled a recluse and hermit. Who cares? He had the right to live his life as he wanted. Besides, he was only labelled a recluse by journalists who were annoyed because he wouldn't talk to them.

Much has been made of his working methods: long hours (he loved film - not many people get a chance to work full-time on something they would do for free); repeated takes (actors often loved the opportunity to refine their role on film, which is not often done in film and, as Kubrick rightly pointed out, if you're paying a couple of million dollars for an actor, you shouldn't worry about spending a couple of hundred dollars on the film stock itself, which is the cheapest part of the process); long periods of filming (Kubrick worked with small crews so there were few overheads); control freak (his attention to detail and perfectionism made him a great film-maker, both artistically and commercially - from *Lolita* onwards, Kubrick gained the respect of film distributors for his groundbreaking statistical research into film theatres and his marketing methods, meaning that commercial success was almost guaranteed).

Stanley Kubrick was the last of the great old-time directors, but this makes him sound as though his films were behind the times, sluggish, doddering. When you watch his films, this is obviously untrue. Kubrick's work, like all masterpieces, has a timeless quality. His vision is so complete, the detail so meticulous, that you believe you are in the three-dimensional space displayed on a two-dimensional screen. What Kubrick has seen, you believe.

1: Eyes Open

On the day Kubrick was born, 26 July 1928, the *New York Times* ran headline stories on boxing (Tunney knocked out Heeney) and Napoleon (manuscripts discovered), two subjects which would forever remain close to his heart. Born into a professional family - his father Jacques was a doctor - they lived in their own house in the Bronx. Jacques gave his son a Graflex camera (one the professionals used), an appreciation of and access to literature and taught him how to play chess - all solitary pursuits, which suited Kubrick's personality.

Pursuing his love of photography, Kubrick would visit neighbour Marvin Traub every five minutes to use his darkroom - they both adored Arthur Fellig, the crime photographer more commonly known as Wee-gee. A rabid movie-goer, a lover of baseball, the only social activity Kubrick indulged was playing the drums in the William Howard Taft High School Band - swing and jazz being his favourite styles.

Photography was an interest which dominated Kubrick's life. He was part of the school club, and often took photos for the school's glossy magazine. Outside of this, Kubrick haunted the streets, developing his eye for a photo. When President Franklin Delano Roosevelt died, Kubrick saw a dejected news vendor surrounded by the headlines - snap, develop, print, Kubrick was off trying to sell it. The best offer came from *Look* magazine, who paid $25 and printed it on 26 June 1945. Kubrick was 17, and graduated into a staff position as full-time photographer for *Look*. He was shown the ropes by the older professionals and eventually got his own byline in January 1949 when *Look* ran 'Prize-fighter,' covering a day in the life of boxer Walter Cartier.

Although it is assumed Kubrick was a loner, this is far from true - he had friends and teachers interested in the same subjects. From high school, he had friends Alexander Singer and Howard O Sackler, and their art teacher Herman Getter introduced them to movie cameras.

Having married high school sweetheart Toba Metz in 1948 and moved to Greenwich Village, Kubrick realised that his true vocation in life was to make films so, with Alex Singer's help, Kubrick began his career as an independent film-maker.

Day Of The Fight (1950)

Cast: Walter Cartier, Douglas Edwards (Narrator), Vincent Cartier, Nate Fleischer

Crew: Director & Producer Stanley Kubrick, Writer Robert Rein, Music Gerald Fried, Editor Julian Bergman, Assistant Director Alexander Singer, 16 minutes

Story: Opening with a newspaper announcing a boxing match, and an accompanying voice-over giving us the low-down on the rough and tumble of the boxing world, we are introduced to a day in the life of the Cartier twins. Walter Cartier is the fighter, and Vincent is the lawyer/manager and former sparring partner in navy and exhibition matches. We first see them wake up after sleeping in the same bed. The camera follows them walking down the street to church and communion. Vincent cooks breakfast for them both. At noon, Walter goes for a check-up, to ensure he is fit and the right weight for the fight, then he eats at a diner. At home, he plays with his dog. Preparing to leave, Walter looks at himself in the mirror, pressing his nose down to see what it would be like broken. After taking a friend's car to the ring, Walter is in a small room, his hands being taped, clasping them, warming up by squatting and punching hands. He is called into the ring, and the fight is on - brutal. Walter knocks out his opponent and wins. It's just another day in the life of a boxer.

Visual Ideas: As the brothers walk down the street, the camera is reverse tracking. There is a diagrammatical look at Walter's equipment on his bed - the camera pans over it from directly above. In the ring, we see Walter sitting on his stool from under his opponent's stool - this gives the impression that Walter is tiny. There is also a great shot from directly under the boxers as they are locked together punching each other.

Audio Idea: Voice-over.

Themes: Symmetry (The Cartier brothers are twins, we see Walter in a mirror); Film Noir (The empty streets, single light source on many shots, especially the church and the waiting room); Hand-To-Hand Fighting (It's about boxing!); Nice To Animals (Walter loves his dog, only it turns out this was not Walter's dog but one Kubrick supplied); Beast In Man (The ever-so-nice Walter turns out to be an animal in the ring); Dancing (In the ring, the two fighters embrace); Theatre/Games (Boxing is both).

Background: Through friend Alex Singer (later a director) who worked at *The March Of Time,* a famous newsreel company, Kubrick found out that they spent $40,000 on each of their short films. Thinking that he could do better, Kubrick used $3,900 of his own money to make *Day Of The Fight.* Using a 100-foot daylight-loading Eyemo camera, and relying on his photojournalism instincts, Kubrick ended up with an interesting film, one that still looks good. The fight itself was filmed using two cameras - one ringside operated by Kubrick, the other in the crowd operated by Singer - with one running whilst the other reloaded. The great shot from under the boxers was Kubrick throwing his hand into the ring and shooting blind hoping it'd come out. Kubrick cut it together and had Singer's friend Gerald Fried put some music to it. When he'd finished, RKO bought the short for a hundred dollars more than Kubrick spent and showed it at the Paramount Theatre in New York. Kubrick took the money because RKO also offered him a $1,500 advance on his next short.

And Another Thing: Walter Cartier appeared in an episode of *Bilko* called *The Boxer.*

The Verdict: Always engrossing, and pretty to look at, it still feels fresh. 4/5

The Flying Padre (1951)

Cast: The Reverend Fred Stadtmueller, Bob Hite (Narrator)

Crew: Director & Writer & Cinematographer Stanley Kubrick, Producer Burton Benjamin, Music Nathaniel Shilkret, Editor Isaac Kleinerman, Sound Harold R Vivian, 8.5 minutes

Story: Two days in the life of the Reverend Fred Stadtmueller who, the voice-over tells us, has 11 churches in four thousand square miles of territory, so he travels by plane. We join Stadtmueller in the air, he performs a burial service, then flies back for mass. Later, a little girl complains about a bully, so the Reverend talks to the boy and tells them to make up. To relax, the Reverend looks after canaries and also enjoys a bit of shooting. Then, an emergency - a woman phones to say her baby is sick, so the Flying Padre flies to collect mother & baby, returning to put them in an ambulance.

Visual Ideas: The close-ups of faces at the funeral are very much like Sergei Eisenstein, famous Russian director (*Battleship Potemkin*, *Ivan The Terrible*), whom Kubrick studied voraciously. Strong light sources in the church. When Stadtmueller is attending his canaries, we see him in silhouette. As he pulls the rotor blades to start the plane, we see his shadow on the ground. Then as he takes off the camera is attached to the wheels so it's very dramatic. The last shot is the best - from the back of an ambulance, which is speeding away, we see the Reverend standing in front of his plane. It's a heroic image, used elsewhere (*Mad Max*, Harry Callaghan in *Dirty Harry*).

Audio Idea: Voice-over.

Themes: Nice To Animals (Stadtmueller loves his canaries); Technology (Kubrick shows the plane from every angle).

Background: Kubrick loved flying - he had got his licence on 15 August 1947 - so this was a good subject for him. Now that he had made his second short film, Kubrick decided that this was what he wanted to do with his life, so he quit his job at *Look*. For a time, Kubrick's only income was $20-£30 a week from playing chess in Washington Square. The game of chess requires logic, order and strategy. Most importantly for Kubrick, it requires the situation to be assessed coolly before moving - an attitude Kubrick brought to his film work.

The Verdict: This is a workmanlike film which shows Kubrick was now a professional film-maker. The fact that it was a human-interest story without much interest is almost missed because it's only 8 minutes long. 2/5

Fear And Desire (1953)

Cast: David Allen (Narrator), Steve Coit (Fletcher), Kenneth Harp (Lt. Corby), Virginia Leith (Girl), Paul Mazursky (Sidney), Frank Silvera (Mac)

Crew: Director & Producer & Cinematographer & Editor Stanley Kubrick, Writers Stanley Kubrick & Howard Sackler, Associate Producer Martin Perveler, Music Gerald Fried, Art Director Herbert Lebowitz, 68 minutes

Story: In an unnamed war, four soldiers survive the crash landing of their plane to find themselves in a forest six miles behind enemy lines. Led by the smug, wisecracking Lt. Corby - he has their only weapon, a pistol - they plan to make their way to a nearby river, build a raft and then, under cover of night, float back to friendly territory. However, when a young woman stumbles across them in the woods, she is assaulted and killed by Sidney, whose mind has gone. An enemy General and his troops are in the vicinity. A confrontation ensues. Whilst Mac is drawing fire, Corby kills the General who looks just like him. Drifting to safety on the raft, Mac is dead, Sidney is still mad, Corby is haunted by himself and Fletcher is numb to all outside stimuli. There's a lot of existential angst.

Visual Style: Eisenstein was Kubrick's first major cinematic influence - in the scene where the soldiers raid the house held by the enemy, Kubrick employs rhythmic jump cuts. Facial close-ups litter the movie.

Audio Style: Beginning and ending with Kubrick's trademark narration, the problem in this case is that the words are pretentious.

Themes: Hand-To-Hand Fighting; The Beast In Man; Staring Eyes; Symmetry (The baddies are played by the same actors who play the goodies).

Subtext: War is Hell, Goddammit!

Background: The earnest script (for example, it contains obtuse references to Shakespeare's *The Tempest*) was written by Howard O Sackler, who later won a Pulitzer Prize for his play *The Great White Hope*. Kubrick got his rich uncle Martin Perveler to put up around $9,000 for *The Trap*, as it was first called, and they were up and running. He cast Frank Silvera, having seen him in Elia Kazan's *Viva Zapata!* with Marlon Brando. For technical back-up, Kubrick asked along Union Carbide executive Steve Hahn because he knew about electricity, and Bob Dierks, an assistant from *Look*, came along to set up and break down equipment. Toba acted as secretary and did the accounts. Sackler asked a 20-year-old student named Paul Mazursky to try out for the role of Sidney. Mazursky went on to direct such films as *Bob & Carol & Ted & Alice* (1969), *Moscow On The Hudson* (1984) and *Down & Out In Beverley Hills* (1986). Mazursky flew with Kubrick, the other actors and the small crew to the San Gabriel Mountains outside Los Angeles, where they met a few Mexicans who were helping to transport the equipment. They were 13 in total - a lucky number Kubrick thought. (In fact, Kubrick made 13 feature films in total.)

Kubrick maintained control of every aspect of production and finance. It looked great - he wanted a fog, so he had a crop sprayer drop insecticide over the location and it almost killed everyone. He decided to film without sound, to speed up the location work, but when they finished shooting Kubrick found that post-synching sound added $30,000 to the cost. The title changed to *The Shape Of Fear* and then became *Fear And Desire* for its première on 26 March 1953. Independent distributor, Joseph Burstyn, who had brought the films of Roberto Rossellini, Victorio De Sica and Jean Renoir to America, booked the movie on the art house circuit, but it never made its money back. The only positive thing Kubrick had to say about the film was that it showed him that films were not very difficult to make, and you did not need too many people either.

And Another Thing: The amateurish and pretentious feel to this movie led Kubrick to hinder public showings of it in later years. However, a print was found and restored, leading to a 1991 showing at the Telluruide Film Festival and then a 1994 public showing (against Kubrick's wishes) at Film Forum in New York. It is still unavailable.

The Verdict: Hey, this is his first movie. Give him a break - the kid had to learn somewhere.

The Seafarers (1953)

Cast: Dan Hollenbeck (Narrator)

Crew: Director & Cinematographer & Editor & Sound Stanley Kubrick, Writer Will Chasen, Producer Lester Cooper, 30 minutes

Background: This industrial film for the Seafarers International Union is remarkable only because it was directed by Kubrick in June 1953. There are shots of ships, machinery, a naked woman (from a barbershop calendar - obviously put in to keep the union members' attention), a canteen and a union meeting. It's in colour, 30 minutes long and was supervised by the staff of *The Seafarer's Log*, the union magazine.

Killer's Kiss (1955)

Cast: Frank Silvera (Vincent Rapallo), Jamie Smith (Davy Gordon), Irene Kane (Gloria Price), Jerry Jarret (Albert, the Fight Manager), Mike Dana (Gangster), Felice Orlandi (Gangster), Ralph Roberts (Gangster), Phil Stevenson (Gangster), Ruth Sobotka (Iris), Julius Adelman (Owner of Mannequin Factory)

Crew: Director & Cinematographer & Editor Stanley Kubrick, Writers Stanley Kubrick (story) & Howard Sackler (uncredited), Producers Morris Bousel & Stanley Kubrick, Music Gerald Fried, 67 minutes

Story: As a man waits at a train station for his girl, he tells us about the recent past and we segue into a long flashback… A morning newspaper announces a big boxing match that night with Davy Gordon. It's his big comeback fight. We see Davy going through his daily routine in his small apartment - he sees a beautiful woman in the apartment opposite. Collecting his mail, Davy reads it on the way to the boxing stadium, thinking of home life. Gloria Price, the girl in the other apartment, is also making her way to work in Times Square, where she is a taxi dancer. As she dances, the owner Vincent Rapallo becomes jealous of the men dancing with her, cuts in and almost starts a fight over Gloria. Vincent and Gloria dance and he takes her to his office where they watch the boxing match on TV. Vincent and Gloria wrestle in front of TV, Vincent trying to kiss Gloria, whilst Davy fights to win his bout. Vincent kisses Gloria as Davy is knocked out because of his glass jaw.

That night, Davy has a nightmare and wakes to Gloria's scream. He rushes around to her room and she explains to Davy that Vincent loves her and he tried to make love to her in her room. She thinks Vincent smells. She falls asleep and Davy spends the night in her room, protecting her. The following morning over breakfast, Gloria tells a story about her father (who became ill and died) and her sister (a ballerina, who married a rich man to look after her father, but when her father died, she died). Davy kisses Gloria and they decide to leave together - Gloria goes to the dance hall to collect her wages and Davy arranges to meet Albert (his manager) outside the hall to be paid for the fight. Seeing Davy waiting for Gloria, Vincent becomes jealous and refuses to give Gloria her money. An argument ensues. Whilst Gloria is talking to Vincent, some conventioneers steal Davy's scarf and he goes running after them. When Gloria returns to the street, Albert (whom Gloria does not know) is waiting and they stand side by side. Vincent's thugs arrive, tell Gloria that she can collect her money and mistakenly assume Albert is Davy. Albert is killed in a back alley, while Gloria and Davy return to their apartments to pack.

When Davy goes to collect Gloria from her room, she has disappeared. He sees the cops enter his room and talk about his manager Albert being killed. Davy takes his gun out of his bags and goes after Vincent by taxi, eventually catching up with Vincent at traffic lights. They are travelling the same roads as those in Davy's nightmare - the nightmare becomes reality.

Arriving at the loft where Vincent and his thugs have Gloria captive, Davy has the villains at gunpoint. As he tries to untie Gloria, one of the thugs throws playing cards at Davy and they overpower him. To save Davy, Gloria gives herself to Vincent. Using this distraction, Davy throws himself through the window and lands safely (from how many floors up?) There follows an impressively photographed long chase through derelict streets and across rooftops, ending in a mannequin warehouse. Vincent and Davy fight - although Vincent has an axe, Davy kills him with a mannequin leg.

The flashback over, we return to Davy at the train station, wondering if Gloria will meet him. As Davy walks towards his train, Gloria arrives and they kiss.

Visual Ideas: From *Day Of The Fight*, Kubrick took the opening shot of the newspaper, the fight preparations in the back room, greasing up like Cartier, the shot of Cartier looking in the mirror to see what his nose looks like when broken, a diagrammatical shot of women's clothes is similar to the shot of Cartier's equipment before he leaves for the fight, the through-the-stool shot, the shot under the fighters as they slug it out. The fighting scenes in this and *Day Of The Fight* look like influences on Martin Scorsese's *Raging Bull* (1980). Kubrick links Davy and Gloria visually - they have the same type of apartment with a window looking at each other, they have photos of home to help them remember the past, they are both paid to 'dance' with a partner on a rectangular piece of floor. The first time we see Davy in his room, there is a knife on the wall, which gives a visual warning that things may go wrong. Also, we see Davy's distorted face through the glass of the fish tank. When Gloria sleeps, Kubrick cuts to a doll in the same position - a bit like Sergei Eisenstein, who often tried to find a visual metaphor for his characters. Davy looks around, touches her tights, sees Gloria in the mirror. When Gloria tells Davy about her father and sister, we go to a close-up of photos of them, and then we see the ballerina perform for the duration of the story. When characters move through the streets, Kubrick places them in one part of the frame and keeps them there whilst the background revolves around them. For example, when Gloria is walking the streets, and when Davy runs after the conventioneers who stole his scarf. The idea of the painting laughing at a character is one that previously appeared in Alfred Hitchcock's *Blackmail* (1929). At the loft, when Davy is in control, Kubrick shows everybody's position, what they see and think just through his cutting - a masterly piece of editing. Just afterwards, Kubrick repeats this trick through editing when Davy considers jumping through a window to escape. In the mannequin warehouse, Vincent is looking for Davy, and we see Davy's head as one of three faces in a row - the other two being mannequins. Just after, a mannequin's hand is directly above Davy, pointing to him, visually telling Vincent where Davy is hiding. When they fight, Davy throws bodies at Vincent, like a bizarre parody of a boxing match. When Vincent starts wielding an axe, one cannot help but be reminded of Jack Nicholson wielding an axe in Kubrick's *The Shining* (1980).

Audio Ideas: Voice-over (The film starts with a voice-over at the train station, when Davy reads his letter on the train, Gloria telling Davy about Vincent loving her and then later the story of her father and sister). During the chase sequence at the end, we hear the sound of drums to give a rhythm, foghorns from the bay to give atmosphere and a telephone ringing to give a sense of urgency. When Vincent is killed with a mannequin's leg, he screams, we cut to a mannequin's mouth, and then to a train whistle and Davy waiting at the train station - this is very much a Hitchcock device.

Themes: Mirrors (Davy looks in his mirror at his apartment. His letter box is mirrored. After the fight Davy is in front of his mirror talking on the phone to a friend and when he says "say look" we see Gloria undressing in the mirror. When Gloria is asleep Davy looks at her in her mirror. Vincent smashes a mirror in a rage. Gloria's reflection is seen in the steel cladding on the dance hall stairway); Corridors (Davy's nightmare, shown in negative, is him travelling through corridor-like streets); Symmetry (The thugs walk towards Albert from either side, giants compared to the tiny figure of Albert in the centre); Film Noir/Expressionism (As Albert is being killed by the two thugs, his arms are up in the air, as though he were caught in the web of shadows behind him); Hand-Held (Most of the scenes around Times Square feel hand-held, like a documentary, but everything else feels very smooth and considered); Hand-To-Hand (Boxing match); Nice To Animals (Davy feeds his goldfish); Dancing (Gloria is a taxi dancer, her sister was a ballerina and Davy dances in the ring); Staring Eyes (Vincent has a tendency to stare and Davy stares into the mirror at the beginning, but nothing in this film is as powerful as later stares); Theatre (The boxing match, the dance hall and the ballet are all kinds of theatres); Games (Cards); Masks/Disguise (Davy's face is distorted when seen through the goldfish bowl); Artificial Bodies (The mannequins are used as a hiding place and as weapons); Family Relationships (As Gloria recounts the story of her father and sister, there are undertones of incest in that relationship, but also guilt on Gloria's part for not being a good daughter, so she punishes herself by becoming a taxi dancer).

Subtext: This is a film about puppets and control. Gloria is a dancing puppet of Vincent's. Her sister was a dancing puppet of her father's. Davy has a choice between Gloria (who represents a home and family) or boxing (where he lives a soulless existence). Visually, we see there are two sides to everything, because we look through mirrors for most of the film. Setting the climax in a mannequin warehouse emphasises the puppet theme. Unfortunately, the bad acting and bad script, help to subsume any such subtle messages, so we end up with a superb-looking melodrama.

Background: Fear And Desire had not made its money back so Kubrick was loathe to go back to the investors and ask for more money on his next project, a film noir he had written with Sackler about a Walter Cartier-like boxer and a taxi dancer who were fighting for survival. Instead, Bronx pharmacist Morris Bousel put up $40,000, and Kubrick was off again. Variously called *The Nymph And The Maniac* and *Kiss Me, Kill Me*, it was a non-union film and they didn't have permission to film on the streets of New York. So, filming on Wall Street in the early hours, Kubrick and his crew found themselves surrounded by policemen. Kubrick was prepared - he handed out $20 bills to each of them and carried on filming. There was also some night shooting on Times Square - using hidden cameras Kubrick got some great footage of people's genuine reaction to the antics of the cast. He also hid a camera in a moving van and got some nice shots of the cast walking through the crowds. Ironically, *Look*'s competitor, *Life* magazine, did a photo-story about the filming. After the debacle of *Fear And Desire*, Kubrick decided to record the sound on location. However, when he set up the lights for filming, he found that the microphones cast all sorts of unwanted shadows. Unable to solve the lighting problems, Kubrick decided to film without sound once again. After the 12-14 week shoot Kubrick had to spend 4 months and an extra $35,000 to add the sound. He got around having to show lengthy dialogue sequences by using voice-overs. For example, in one scene, a long story is told whilst watching a ballet dancer. The dancer was Ruth Sobotka, a dancer with the New York City Ballet, with whom Kubrick was living at the time. They married on 15 January 1955.

Legacies: Killer's Kiss is the basis for *Strangers Kiss* (1984, director Matthew Chapman). Set in 1955, it is the story of film director Stanley (Peter Coyote) who is directing a noirish film about a boxer trying to save a taxi dancer from an over-attentive boss i.e. he's directing *Killer's Kiss*. The actress is falling in love with the actor, much to the annoyance of her boyfriend, the rich realtor financing the film. Coyote tries to manipulate the situation so that the real emotions on show get into the film. Fascinating, it works on many levels and is well worth checking out.

The Verdict: As technically accomplished and stylish as *Killer's Kiss* is, Kubrick hasn't got inside the heads of his characters to show us their emotions. 2/5

2: Eyes Peeled

Kubrick regarded *Killer's Kiss* as nothing more than an accomplished student film and was looking for future opportunities. During the Korean War, Alex Singer was in the Signal Corps with James B Harris where they plotted future careers in the movies. Harris and Singer hooked up together to make a film, inspired by the way Kubrick had got his two shorts and two features made, but nothing came of it. Eventually, Harris and Kubrick got together, agreeing that if Harris produced then it would give Kubrick more freedom to direct. Harris immediately went to the bookstore to look for a property for them to film. He saw a copy of *Clean Break* by Lionel White, a novel about a racetrack robbery. 'This seems exciting,' Harris thought.

The Killing (1956)

Cast: Sterling Hayden (Johnny Clay), Coleen Gray (Fay), Vince Edwards (Val Cannon), Jay C Flippen (Marvin Unger), Ted de Corsica (Randy Kennan), Marie Windsor (Sherry Peatty), Elisha Cook Jr. (George Peatty), Joe Sawyer (Mike O'Reilly), James Edwards (Parking Attendant), Timothy Carey (Nikki Arane), Kola Kwariani (Maurice Oboukhoff), Jay Adler (Leo Tito Vuolo), Joe Turkel (Tiny)

Crew: Director Stanley Kubrick, Writers Stanley Kubrick & Jim Thompson (dialogue), Novel *Clean Break* Lionel White, Producer James B Harris, Associate Producer Alexander Singer, Music Gerald Fried, Cinematographer Lucien Ballard, Editor Betty Steinberg, Art Director Ruth Sobotka, 85 minutes

Working Titles: Bed Of Fear, Day Of Violence

Story: Saturday, 3.45pm - Drunk Marvin Unger is at a racetrack. He passes an address and time to the barman, and then to a cashier. 2.45pm - Randy, a policeman, meets a man to extend his loan of $3,000, which he promises will be repaid shortly. 7.00pm - Johnny Clay, who has just done a 5-year stretch, tells his girlfriend Fay that he is going for the big one, and he's going to use non-criminals. 6.30pm - Mike O'Reilly, the racetrack bartender, returns home to his sick wife for whom he wants the best. 7.15pm - George Peatty, the racetrack cashier, returns home to his mean, sarcastic wife, Sherry. George is a wimp who loves his wife, but she wants a real man and one with money to boot. When George lets it slip that he'll soon have all the money she could wish for, Sherry whee-dles information out of him about the upcoming racetrack heist. Cut to Sherry meeting her lover Val Cannon and their plan to take all the money for themselves. Cut to the gang (Johnny, Randy, George, Mike, Marvin) meeting at 8.00pm as arranged and Johnny, the leader, explain-ing that he will hire 2 professionals, a shooter and a fighter, to carry out vital parts of the plan, reassuring them that the professionals are on a fixed fee and do not get a share of the estimated $2 million. Marvin put up the money for them. Johnny hears a noise - it's a woman, Sherry, whom he knocks out. George starts whining, Randy hits him and the whole plan looks compromised. Johnny has a talk with Sherry, says that he knows she's only interested in money but if she keeps her mouth shut she'll get a bundle. When George and Sherry return home, George wants to call the whole thing off but Sherry persuades him to continue with the plan.

Tuesday, 10.15am - At the Chess Academy, Johnny persuades his friend Maurice Oboukhoff, wrestler and chess master, to start a fight at the racetrack for $2,500. Next he visits professional shooter Nikki Arane. They test the gun Johnny is to use for the robbery, then Johnny asks Nikki if he could shoot a horse, Red Lightning, in the 7th race, for $5,000, no questions asked. Nikki agrees. Finally, Johnny gets a motel room from Leo Tito Vuolo, the father of a prison friend. Johnny leaves a package in the motel room.

Saturday, 7.30am - George is up early, wide awake, so Sherry sus-pects the robbery will be today. She pretends Johnny raped her the previ-ous week to make George angry enough to tell her the plan. 5.00am - Johnny tells Marvin to stay away from the track, but Marvin sees Johnny as his son and wants to protect him. 7.00am - At the airport Johnny buys flight tickets for Fay and himself for 9pm that night. 8.15am - Johnny goes to the motel, via a florist, and transfers the gun from his package into the flower box. 8.45am - At the bus station, Johnny puts the flower box in a locker. 9.20am - Johnny drops the locker key into Mike's letter box. 11.15am - Mike gets ready for work, attends to his sick wife and collects the locker key. 11.29am - Mike collects the flower box from the bus station and gets on the bus to the racetrack. 12.10pm - Mike at the racetrack locker room, gets changed for work and puts the flower box in his locker. Nearby, George gets a small gun and hides it on his person. We follow Mike to his bar and, as the first race is announced, Marvin turns up drunk. 3.32pm - Randy reports to his superior that his radio is on the blink. He is on schedule, heading for the racetrack. At the race-track, he leans on his car, arms folded, looking up at an open window, listening to the 7th race, the $100,000 Lansdowne Stakes, start. 2.30pm - Maurice leaves his chess club for the track and, as the 7th race starts, he starts a big fight, distracting the police, and drawing the police out of the money room. As he fights, George opens the security door, Johnny slips in and Maurice is dragged away at 4.23pm. 11.40am - Nikki leaves his farm in his fast car. 12.30pm - Nikki is at the track car park and, by pre-tending to have a wooden leg, bribes the attendant (who has a wooden leg) into letting him have the spot he wants. At the 7th race, the horses are off, Nikki prepares, shoots Red Lightning, reverses the car, punc-tures a tyre on a horseshoe and is shot by the attendant. 4.24pm - Nikki dies. 2.15pm - Johnny is in the city, making his way to the racetrack. As the 7th race is announced, Johnny sees Marvin drunk, then waits by the security door as Maurice begins his fight. The guards come through the door and Johnny is let in by George. In the locker room, he takes the rifle, puts on a mask and gloves, then takes a sack, knocks on the money room door, enters, holds 3 men hostage as one of them fills the sack, puts all the men in the locker room, takes off his outer clothes, stuffs them (and gun) into the sack and throws the sack out the window. As he comes out through the security door a policeman stops Johnny. Marvin bumps him and Johnny knocks him out. Later that evening, Randy, George, Mike and Marvin gather and listen to the radio report. (We see that the bag came out the window, landed at Randy's feet - he took the money and left it in the motel room.) Val and a friend crash in, George starts shooting and everybody dies except George, who is badly wounded. 6.25pm - Johnny, with the money in his car, sees George cov-ered with blood as he leaves the hotel so assumes something has gone wrong. Johnny buys the largest suitcase he can find and fills it with the money. Meanwhile, George returns home to find Sherry packing - she betrayed him - and shoots her. George falls dead, their pet parrot lying in the cage beside him. At the airport, Fay is waiting for Johnny. Plain-clothes police detectives are in the background, as Johnny arrives. At the check-in, Johnny tries to bring the suitcase on the plane as hand luggage, but the assistant will not let him - after an argument, Johnny agrees to check it in. Outside, waiting to board, as the plane taxis, a pet dog runs into the path of the luggage truck, which swerves. The suitcase tumbles, flips open and the money is flown into the air, like confetti, by the wind created by the airplane engine. Johnny, in shock, is led out of the airport by Fay. A taxi leaves as they arrive at the front. They hail more taxis but each of them simply goes past. Two policemen slowly walk up to them.

Visual Ideas: Mirrors (Kubrick doesn't use physical mirrors, but he shows the same events from different angles, and at different times, giving a refracted effect); Film Noir/Expressionism (Virtually every shot in this dark film uses single source lighting, or puts layers of intricate shadows over the faces, or plunges the background into black); Hand-Held (Kubrick holds the camera as, from George's point of view, we see all the dead bodies); Circles (The racetrack, the circular lights dotted throughout the film); Reverse Tracking (When Johnny walks into the bus station, and later Mike walks into it); Numbers (Since this is about money, there are many numbers on windows and signs throughout the film).

Audio Ideas: Voice-over (The whole movie is dotted with an authoritative, documentary-type voice telling us times and dates and motivation); Overlapping Dialogue (The rhythm of dialogue and voice-over is like a waltz ebbing and flowing, mesmeric).

Themes: Hand-To-Hand (Johnny hitting the policeman, Maurice throwing the police around); Nice To Animals (Nikki has a puppy he strokes affectionately. George & Sherry have a parrot); Staring/Eyes (When George is shot, and he returns home to his wife, his eyes stare, shocked, in pain, before he shoots his wife); Theatre (Maurice is an ex-wrestler and puts on a performance at the racetrack's bar as a diversion); Games (Betting horses. Chess. At the very beginning the voice-over says that Marvin is playing his part in the jigsaw as we see him discard his losing tickets on the floor of the betting office, which is littered with thousands of losing tickets. Later we see the dead bodies of our main characters, littering the floor like those losing tickets); Masks/Disguise (Johnny wears a mask when he commits the robbery. Sherry puts on and takes off her make-up when she's persuading George to do things for her); Drinking Bars (Long walks to the bar); Artificial Bodies (The human targets on the shooting range when Nikki is practising); The Paralysed Man/Illness (Mike's wife is ill. Nikki pretends to have a wooden leg to get a parking place. The parking attendant has a wooden leg); The Collapse Of Society (Society does not prevent crime or aid the capture of criminals. Fate and its younger brother irony gang up on the criminals. The policeman, a trusted member of society, is a criminal. The cashier and barman are both committing a crime for their wives);

Family Relationships (Mike looks after his sick wife in the same way that Gloria's sister, in *Killer's Kiss*, looks after her dying father).

Subtext: Like John Huston's *The Asphalt Jungle* (1950, based on the novel by W R Burnett, also starring Sterling Hayden) and other heist movies, this is a meticulous step-by-step, chess-like explanation of how everything that man does is doomed to failure and is self-destructive. Johnny spends the whole of the movie trying to achieve something, but it is all for nothing. It is succinctly summed up by Johnny's last words in the film, "What's the difference?" We all end up as food for the worms, so why bother trying to do anything at all? The fact that this is a crime movie makes this 'moral' ending acceptable to viewers because the bad men get caught, but the hidden message is that these bad men represent ordinary people - the law enforcer (Randy), the accountant (George), the labourer (Mike), the intellectual/artist (Maurice), the fighter (Nikki), the waster (Marvin) and the gangster (Johnny). This is pointed up when Maurice (artist) makes the direct connection whilst talking to Johnny (gangster) at the chess club, "I often thought that the gangster and the artist are the same in the eyes of the masses. They are admired and hero-worshipped, but there is always present an underlying wish to see them destroyed at the peak of their glory."

Background: Harris and Kubrick loved the novel *Clean Break* because of the way it presented multiple points of view in fragmented slices of time. Kubrick had already played with this idea in *Killer's Kiss*, but here was a solid story with solid characters. Harris approached the agents to buy the rights and found out that United Artists were interested in the property for Frank Sinatra - as a follow-on to the successful thriller *Suddenly* (1954, director Lewis Allen, script Richard Sale). But Sinatra was dragging his heels over whether or not to do *Clean Break*, so Harris asked how much they wanted for the rights - $10,000 - and sent the cheque.

Kubrick then suggested that they get novelist Jim Thompson to write the script. Thompson had written more than 10 great noir paperback originals for Lion since 1952 including *The Killer Inside Me* (1952, for which Kubrick later supplied the quote, "Probably the most chilling and believable first-person story of a criminally warped mind I have ever encountered"), *Savage Night* (1953), *A Hell Of A Woman* (1954) and *After Dark, My Sweet* (1955). The fractured time structure from the novel was used. Kubrick decided which scenes were to be included and the purpose of each scene. Thompson went to his room and wrote it up.

Thompson added Mike's ailing wife, the wrestler's speech about gangsters & artists and the sadomasochistic relationship between George and Sherry. The novel ends with George shooting Johnny, but there were lots of alternative endings for the movie - one had Johnny go after the money as it swirled about only to get chopped up by the engine propellers. Of course, the ending they used owes more than a little to the ending of *The Treasure Of The Sierra Madre* (1948, director John Huston, novel B Traven).

Script completed, they were told by United Artists that if Harris-Kubrick got a big actor, UA would put up some money. Copies were mailed to every leading actor and Sterling Hayden (the police chief in *Suddenly* and the lead in *The Asphalt Jungle*) said he'd do it for $40,000. UA put up $200,000, Harris put up $80,000 and loaned $50,000 from his father - the film was financed.

Kubrick, Harris and Singer moved from New York to LA for location work and filming interiors in Charlie Chaplin's studios. Kubrick worked for free, living off loans from Harris, whilst his wife Ruth, who had designed ballets and stage productions, designed the sets and drew storyboards of the film. Union rules said that Kubrick could not be the cinematographer, so veteran Lucien Ballard was brought in. Kubrick sent him out with several cameras and a crew of ten to film second unit material of the races at Bay Meadow Racetrack. He returned with thousands of feet of useless footage. Ballard was a Hollywood man and was used to controlled conditions - he did not know how to light or deal with spontaneous subjects. Instead, Kubrick sent Alex Singer, an experienced photojournalist, with a hand-held Eyemo and a couple of hundred feet of film to do the job over a weekend. Singer's footage was used throughout the movie with his most spectacular shot - the horses leaving the starting gate and galloping towards us - saved until last.

For the interiors, there was a big set with the cashier windows (each name on the windows an in-joke), security door and bar. Kubrick set up a long tracking shot - his trademark - for Johnny's apartment, where Johnny walks through several rooms and we go through the walls. Kubrick set the camera close to the actors, and used a 25mm wide angle lens which would give great clarity, intimacy with the actors and a slight distortion, making it a dynamic shot. Whilst Kubrick's back was turned, Ballard set it up with a 50mm lens and moved the camera a long way from the actors. Quietly, calmly, Kubrick - who was still only 27 - told Ballard to move the camera back or he was off the set. Kubrick had acquired the quiet authority which allowed him to dominate a set without resorting to histrionics. The actors said that to direct them, he would take them aside individually, say a few words and then return to the shot. This was a man who treated each person as an individual.

Filming went to plan but at the preview, agents and friends advised Kubrick that the manipulation of time was too confusing and that he should recut it to straighten the story. Kubrick took the film to New York for recutting but decided against it, making the decision that the time fragmentation was the reason they had bought the rights to the novel in the first place. *The Killing* failed to get a proper release and was put in at the last minute playing second feature to *Bandido!* (1956, director Richard Fleischer). It didn't make any money but it did get some favourable reviews. One critic compared it to Orson Welles' *Citizen Kane* (1941), citing the distortion of time and the deep focus photography as being similar.

Legacies: Quentin Tarantino used the fractured-time technique in *Reservoir Dogs* (1991), *Pulp Fiction* (1994) and *Jackie Brown* (1997).

The Verdict: Although this has the format of a true crime article turned into a documentary film, it has added depth because of the great cast of noir characters and the actors playing them. Every single one of them - dignified Kola Kwariani, slimy Timothy Carey, tough Ted de Corsica, wimp Elisha Cook Jr., vamp Marie Windsor - plays a vital part in bringing it alive. Kubrick's cold, detached, Godlike eye watches them destroy themselves and each other. It's cool. 4/5

Paths Of Glory (1957)

Cast: Kirk Douglas (Colonel Dax), Ralph Meeker (Corporal Paris), Adolphe Menjou (General Broulard), George Macready (General Mireau), Wayne Morris (Lieutenant Roget), Richard Anderson (Major Saint-Auban), Timothy Carey (Private Férol), Joe Turkel (Private Arnaud), Susanne Christian (German Singer), Bert Freed (Sergeant Boulanger), John Stein (Captain Rousseau), Ken Dibbs (Private Lejeune)

Crew: Director Stanley Kubrick, Writers Stanley Kubrick & Jim Thompson & Calder Willingham, Novel Humphrey Cobb, Producer James B Harris, Music Gerald Fried, Cinematographer George Krause, Editor Eva Kroll, Art Director Ludwig Reiber, Military Advisor Baron von Waldendels, 86 minutes

Story: France 1916: The French have been at war with the Germans since 3 August 1914 and now warfare is reduced to trenches where gains are measured in feet and inches instead of miles. At a luxurious château, General Paul Mireau is explaining to his superior, General George Broulard, that he likes to create a pleasant atmosphere in which to work. George explains that the anthill - fortified German trenches overlooking the French trenches - has to be taken and hints that a promotion could be in the offing. Paul talks about the good health of his brave men and then persuades himself that yes, the anthill may be impregnable but his men are brave and, yes, they could take it.

In the mud trenches we see General Mireau doing morale work, issuing clichés to his men. When he meets a shell-shocked soldier, Mireau insists that there is no such thing as shell-shock. His aide, Major Saint-Auban, sucks up to him like the little toady he is. They meet Colonel Dax, who is washing the mud off himself, symbolically becoming an officer. When Saint-Auban and Dax talk we discover that Saint-Auban thinks of the soldiers as lower animals and Dax thinks of them as humans. General Mireau says that Dax's men are to take the anthill the following morning. Only 40% of Dax's men are expected to live. Dax is outraged. Mireau says it is for France. Dax quotes Samuel Johnson, "Patriotism is the last refuge of the scoundrel" - an insult to Mireau, which is ignored because Dax has to lead his troops out to battle.

That night, Dax sends three men out on a reconnaissance mission into no man's land to prepare for the morning assault: Lieutenant Roget, Corporal Paris and Private Lejeune. When they see a crashed plane, Roget sends Lejeune to investigate - Paris protests because a night patrol should never be separated. Whilst waiting Roget the coward becomes nervous, throws a grenade and runs. Paris investigates and finds Lejeune dead by the Lieutenant's grenade. Returning to the trench, Paris accuses Roget of murder, but there are no witnesses and whom would people believe - an officer or a soldier?

Morning. Dax walks through the trenches, looking at the men, as the barrage throws tons of dirt up into the air and down into the trenches. Then, on time, Dax blows his whistle and goes over the top. Wave upon wave of men follow him, running, jumping through wire, diving into craters, shredded by wire, bullets, bombs. "Where's B Company?" Dax asks, and goes back to find them. From afar, General Mireau sees B Company, led by the coward Roget, still in their trenches. Angry, he orders them to be bombed. Battery commander Captain Rousseau

31

refuses to kill his own men without written orders. Livid with rage, Mireau tells Rousseau to report for a court martial. The attack on the ant-hill fails and the soldiers retreat.

Mireau, Dax and Broulard meet to discuss the attack. Mireau thinks all the troops are scum and wants to kill 100 of them as an example. Dax argues against this punishment and General Mireau eventually decides on three men, to be picked by the company commanders. Dax disagrees with the whole thing and says that if an example has to be made, shoot him. Broulard coolly replies, "It isn't a matter of officers." Dax says he will defend the men - he used to be a trial lawyer. As Mireau leaves with Broulard, Captain Rousseau arrives for his court martial but Mireau gets rid of him so that he is not embarrassed in front of his superior.

Three men are picked: Arnaud, Férol and Paris. Paris explains that he was picked purely because he saw Roget kill Lejeune. Dax tells them it is unfair and gives them instructions about how to act in court.

At the general court martial, held in a large ballroom within the châ-teau, each man is presented in turn, Major Saint-Auban prosecuting, Colonel Dax defending. The indictment is not read out because it would waste time. Dax protests at the absurdity of the court martial, that there are no witnesses for the prosecution, that there is no stenographer mak-ing a record of the trial. "To find these men guilty would be a crime," Dax shouts.

Evening. The prisoners in their stable prison, get a luxurious meal from General Mireau, but it is drugged so they do not eat. Getting des-perate, they try to think of a way of escaping. The priest arrives and tells them the bad news - Dax has tried to interest officers at headquarters but nobody there wants to know. The three men realise their plight is hope-less, they are lost. Férol becomes depressed and turns to God. Arnaud becomes angry and goes wild. Paris hits Arnaud to quieten him, but Arnaud falls backwards, hits his head and cracks his skull. Unconscious, Sergeant Boulanger pinches Arnaud's cheeks saying, "The General wants him awake when he is shot."

Rousseau informs Dax of General Mireau's order to bomb B Com-pany. Next, Dax summons Roget and tells him he is to command the fir-ing squad.

In the château, in the ballroom, officers and women are eating and drinking, dancing to waltz music. Dax and Broulard retire to the library alone. Broulard tells Dax that, looking over the records, his men must have fought bravely to have suffered so many casualties. If so, Dax counters, why should three more die? Can't the General Staff reconsider? Broulard points out that the General Staff have come under criticism from politicians and the press and someone must take the blame - the death of three more men will bolster the troops, make them try harder next time. Dax asks Broulard if he really believes what he's saying. As they leave the library - Dax asks if General Broulard was aware of Mireau's order to fire on his own troops and presents written testimony from several witnesses.

Morning. The prisoners walk between two long rows of soldiers in dress parade, drums beating. Paris is still defiant, Férol is pleading for his life to the priest, Arnaud is unconscious on a stretcher. Dax looks on angry, the Generals are impassive. The prisoners are tied to the poles, the priest blesses them and Roget offers a blindfold to each of them (and says sorry to Paris). The firing squad (eight per man) get ready, aim, fire.

The two Generals are eating. "The men died wonderfully," Mireau comments, "There is always a chance that one will do something that will leave a bad taste in your mouth." As Dax enters, Broulard informs Mireau of the enquiry into the order to bomb B Company. His career ruined, Mireau storms out. Broulard calmly offers Dax Mireau's command, since he assumed that was Dax's motive. When he realises Dax really did want to save the men, Broulard pities Dax for his idealism and sentimentality.

Dax goes past a hall where the men are drinking. The owner introduces a German girl. The men laugh and jeer at her but when she sings a German folk song its purity touches them and they begin humming the tune with her. Dax is touched - he realises that this simple humanity is what he is fighting for.

Visual Ideas: Corridors (Trenches. As the prisoners walk to their execution, they are in a corridor of soldiers); Symmetry (During the trial, because it is a formal event, the prisoners and the judges are seen as a row of people, giving a sense of symmetry. During the execution ceremony, also a formal event, the soldiers on parade are arranged symmetrically in front of the château); Film Noir/Expressionism (The night patrol); Circles (In the opening scene Broulard takes Mireau by the arm and leads him around the room, in a circle, like a dance); Reverse Tracking (The walks through the trenches are shown from the characters' point of view and as reverse tracking). The walks of Mireau and Dax through the trenches are from left to right which, psychologically, is very strong, whereas the raid on the anthill is relentlessly from right to left, psychologically very weak, as though going uphill. The relentless walking and being killed, and it never seeming to stop, remind me of the landing on Normandy beach in *Saving Private Ryan* (1998, director Steven Spielberg).

Audio Ideas: Voice-over (The introduction); The Waltz (After the prisoners are sentenced, and while they eat nothing in prison because the food is drugged, the officers eat from a large table and dance a waltz in the room where the court martial was held).

Themes: Hand-To-Hand (Paris and Arnaud fight in prison): Not Nice To Animals (The soldiers are treated like animals, living underground. Saint-Auban talks about herd instinct. The prisoners are kept in a stable); Staring/Eyes (The shell-shocked soldier. Paris just before he hits Arnaud); Theatre (The German girl starts singing at the hall. The court martial is pure theatre and nothing at all to do with justice); Games (They play power games, and with people's lives. The marble floor of the château is chequered like a chessboard so that in the court martial the prisoners are merely pawns); Masks/Disguise (The night patrol put black on their faces. General Mireau has a large scar on his face. Major Saint-Auban is always acting like a sycophant); The 18th Century (The château is from that period); Bars (There's drink at the German hall. The Generals have their own personal supplies always available); Artificial Bodies (It could be argued that virtually everybody outside of Dax and Paris and perhaps Rousseau act out of self-interest. The soldiers are treated like playthings not like people); The Fatal Flaw (Dax will never progress because he believes in people more than in power/self-interest. Mireau is a former soldier, perhaps how Dax will be in the future, whose self-interest is so overpowering that he forgets about politics and loses his job. Paris believes in justice - Roget should be charged - but he has neither the power nor the political clout to do anything about it, so he is killed to be kept quiet); The Paralysed Man/Illness (The shell-shocked man is the only man we see who is injured by the war. Arnaud is so ill he has to be stretchered to the execution); The Collapse Of Society (This is a male society, and it tells us that men are interested in power over other men); Family Relationships (Paris is the only soldier who mentions his family).

Subtext: Man has failed to organise his society to the benefit of man - on the contrary, he is destroying himself. This is an examination of a society where power, politics (the handling of power) and selfishness (the reason why people want power) are paramount. This society destroys everybody that is part of it: the people who do not want to be part of it (Férol, Paris); or want to change it (Dax); or embrace it (Mireau). The only person who seems unaffected by this is Broulard - he represents the society and explains its workings.

Background: Paths Of Glory was the only book Humphrey Cobb wrote. He saw a New York Times newspaper report about five French soldiers shot for mutiny in 1915 - the men were cleared and their widows got 7 cents each. From this, combined with his own experience of World War One, Cobb fashioned the book. The book and film differ in several ways. The first third of the novel deals with the day-to-day life of the three soldiers - something which is not tackled in the film. The tragic events are propelled by an absurd situation. It is reported that the anthill has been taken when it has not. In order not to contradict the report and save face, the anthill is ordered to be taken, which constitutes the second third of the book. When the attack fails, the court martial and execution is carried out in the last third. The book looks at the events from the prisoners' point of view, with hardly any reference to the scheming carried out behind their heads. For example, in the book Colonel Dax does not represent the prisoners at their trial and does not attempt to blackmail Mireau.

Kubrick had read Cobb's 1935 novel one day in his father's waiting room. Impressed by it then, he decided to make it into a movie. During the day they would work with novelist Calder Willingham (fresh off script doctor duties on *The Bridge On The River Kwai* (1957, director David Lean)) on an adaptation of Stefan Zweig's novel *The Burning Secret*, whilst the night was spent getting Jim Thompson to do the first draft of *Paths Of Glory*. The script was rewritten by Calder Willingham. Kirk Douglas, who was riding high on *Lust For Life* (1956, director Vincente Minnelli), wanted to do it. Douglas blackmailed United Artists to take the project by saying he would not do *The Vikings* (1958, Richard Fleischer) unless they took *Paths Of Glory*. UA gave the film a budget of $850,000, of which Douglas got $350,000. On top of that, Douglas' company Bryna Productions would get production credit, and he tied Harris-Kubrick Productions to a five-picture deal - Harris-Kubrick would get about $20,000 between them for their efforts, plus 60% of the profits.

Deals done, the production moved to Munich, Germany, for filming, since problems were anticipated trying to film in France. The château and battlefield were 40 minutes from the studio. Ironically, 800 German policemen, who had undergone strict military training as part of their enrolment, were used to play the battle-weary French soldiers. For the battle scenes, some of which were repeated more than 30 times, new techniques were invented to present realistic explosions, with chunks of earth flying up into the air instead of the usual plume of smoke. Erwin Lange, the technician in charge, had to go in front of a commission to obtain permission to amass so many explosives and more than a ton of them were detonated in the first week.

On the first day of shooting Kubrick told Richard Anderson, who played Saint-Auban and was also script coach for the cast, that Max Ophuls had died, and that this film was for him. Kubrick may well have emulated the fluid camera movements of Ophuls.

When Douglas first arrived on the set, he was given the new script (possibly Jim Thompson's first draft) which he thought was rubbish - it had unrealistic lines and a happy ending! Kubrick's explanation was that he wanted to make a more commercial film, which meant the soldiers got a last-minute reprieve. Douglas threw the script away saying he wanted the draft Willingham worked on (probably because they beefed up the Dax character for Douglas). Douglas got his way.

From the outset, the film caused controversy among the military around the world. It was banned in France. It was withdrawn from the Berlin Film Festival. It was censored by the Swiss Army until 1970. The US military even banned it from its European bases. Otherwise, Italian critics voted it best foreign film of 1958 and Winston Churchill commented on its authenticity. In 1974, *Paths Of Glory* had its first showing to French audiences. Yet again, *Paths Of Glory* was a prestige project, i.e. lots of critics liked it but nobody came to see it, therefore Kubrick did not make any money.

And Another Thing: The German girl, played by Susanne Christian whose real name is Christiane Susanne Harlan, became Kubrick's third wife and lifetime partner.

Legacies: There is a reference to *Paths Of Glory* in François Truffaut's *Vivement Dimanche!* (1983).

The Verdict: A stone classic. Acting, script, photography, explosions etc. are all great, and each time you watch it you become angry at the injustice of it all. 5/5

3: Eyesore

After *Paths Of Glory*, Kubrick worked on several ideas including a sitcom starring Ernie Kovacs, and a film of the book *I Stole $16,000,000* by real-life criminal Herbert Emerson Wilson with a script by Jim Thompson. However, most of his time was spent getting friendly with Marlon Brando and, from 12 May 1958, working on *The Authentic Death Of Hendry Jones*, from a western novel by Charles Neider, based on the story of lawman Pat Garrett and outlaw Billy The Kid, with a first draft script by Sam Peckinpah. Kubrick fired Peckinpah and brought in Calder Willingham for a script rewrite but the changes, which included Brando as the villain becoming the good guy, made it a very messy business. Kubrick did not know what the film was about so quit the project. The title changed to *One-Eyed Jacks* (1961), Marlon Brando directed and, although two of his scenes remained intact, Peckinpah got no credit. Peckinpah went on to direct *Pat Garrett & Billy The Kid* (1973).

Kubrick was 30, had made 4 feature films, had handled movies with budgets up to a million dollars, but he had yet to make a single dollar out of his skill as a director because his income was dependent on profit and none of his films had been profitable.

Meanwhile, Kirk Douglas had found another film to produce where he could play a heroic character with a social conscience: *Spartacus*.

Spartacus (1960)

Cast: Kirk Douglas (Spartacus), Laurence Olivier (Marcus Licinius Crassus), Jean Simmons (Varinia), Charles Laughton (Lentulus Gracchus), Peter Ustinov (Lentulus Batiatus), John Gavin (Julius Caesar), Nina Foch (Helena Glabrus), John Ireland (Crixus), Herbert Lom (Tigranes), John Dall (Glabrus), Charles McGraw (Marcellus), Woody Strode (Draba), Tony Curtis (Antoninus), Anthony Hopkins (voice of Marcus Licinius Crassus in some scenes, 1991 restoration)

Crew: Director Stanley Kubrick, Writers Dalton Trumbo & Calder Willingham (uncredited for battle scenes), Novel Howard Fast, Executive Producer Kirk Douglas, Producer Edward Lewis, Music Alex North, Cinematographers Russell Metty & Clifford Stine (additional scenes), Editor Robert Lawrence, Production Design Alexander Golitzen, Title Designer Saul Bass, Second Unit Director Yakima Canutt, Historical & Technical Advisor Vittorio Nino Novarese, USA première 184 minutes, then released at 161 minutes, 1991 restored version is 198 minutes

Story: Spartacus, a Thracian, born into slavery and sold to the mines of Libya at the age of 13, helps a slave who falls. Spartacus is beaten by Roman guards for his trouble and pegged out on a rock to die. Lentulus Batiatus buys him.

When the slaves return to Capua in Italy, Spartacus finds that he is part of Batiatus' school for gladiators. Former slave and gladiator Marcellus begins training them, picking Spartacus out as a troublemaker. As a reward for his hard work, Batiatus pairs Spartacus with the beautiful Varinia. Later, Marcellus taunts Spartacus by arranging for Varinia to be allocated to another gladiator.

Marcus Licinius Crassus, an important member of the Roman Senate, arrives with some guests, who want a gladiator show performed, to the death. The women pick four men. Spartacus' friend Crixus fights and kills a man. Then it is time for Spartacus and the tall Ethiopian Draba to fight. The women are enraptured whilst the men discuss politics - Crassus gives Glabrus the seal of Commander of the Roman Garrison. Draba defeats Spartacus and is about to kill him when, at the last minute, he hesitates, turns, throws his trident at the visitors and jumps up at them. He gets a javelin in the back. Crassus takes out his dagger and puts it into Draba's back.

The next day, when Spartacus learns that Varinia has been sold to Crassus, he attacks Marcellus and the gladiators follow suit, overpower the guards and escape to the hills. The small army of gladiators begin burning estates and freeing slaves. Meanwhile, at the Senate in Rome, we meet the Republican leader Lentulus Gracchus, sworn enemy of Crassus. It is decided that Glabrus should go to quell the slave revolt, leaving Gracchus' friend Julius Caesar in charge of the Garrison of Rome.

The gladiators, led by Spartacus, take up residence on Mount Vesuvius, where they are joined by thousands of slaves. Varinia and Spartacus are reunited and profess their love for each other. Antoninus also joins - he was Crassus' slave and, when Crassus revealed he was bisexual, Antoninus escaped. As well as performing magic and reciting poems, Antoninus reads and prepares documents for Spartacus. Tigranes, the agent for pirates, agrees that in seven months, 500 pirate ships will be at Brundiusium, a Southern port, to transport the slaves overseas.

The six cohorts led by Glabrus are defeated by the slave army and he is sent home to Rome to report his disgrace. He is exiled by the Senate and, as his sponsor, Crassus is honour-bound to retire to private life.

The slave army marches across Italy in the winter - people die, are injured, suffer hardship - and in the spring Varinia announces her pregnancy.

Rome is in turmoil through lack of food because the slaves are disrupting the food supply. Since there is talk of Crassus leading a Roman army against Spartacus, Gracchus bribes the pirates to ensure they take the slaves thus removing the problem. Just outside Brundiusium, the slaves see the pirate ships waiting and celebrate. Then Tigranes brings bad news - Crassus has paid off the pirates to force a confrontation. And more bad news, Lucullus and his army are arriving at Brundiusium from Asia Minor, so the slave army must march towards Rome and its new dictator, Crassus. The night before the big battle, Spartacus surveys his people, while Crassus plans to "kill the legend of Spartacus."

The battle is long and bloody. Crassus' 20 legions seem to be matched by Spartacus' army, until the army of Lucullus and Pompei mount a surprise attack. It is a slaughter, and 6,000 slaves are captured. Crassus says that if they reveal which of them is Spartacus, then they will be spared crucifixion. Spartacus rises to save their lives but, as he does so, all the slaves rise and identify themselves as Spartacus - Crassus orders them all to be crucified. Spartacus' child was born on the battle-field - he and Varinia are found by Crassus, who takes them for his own.

Crassus orders that Antoninus and Spartacus (Crassus knows he is Spartacus) are the last to be crucified, at the gates to Rome. Then he orders them to fight to the death, so that one is spared the agony of cruci-fixion. In a circle of Roman soldiers Spartacus kills his friend and is then crucified. Meanwhile, Batiatus smuggles Varinia and her child out of Rome with Gracchus' help. On the way out of Rome, Varinia shows Spartacus his son - his son is free.

Visual Ideas: Corridors (The crucifixes lining the Appian Way); Symmetry (When we go to Rome, Kubrick often puts in a symmetrical shot to show order); Film Noir/Expressionism (When the gladiators are in their cells, the harsh lights are very expressionistic. Also, in the slaves' camp at night, Spartacus is often lit with a blue light on one side (for the moon) and a yellow light on the other, to show his inner con-flict); Circles (The fight arena when the gladiators are fighting for Cras-sus. When Glabrus and his cohorts are overthrown, the Roman commander stands inside a circle of rebels. At the end, Spartacus fights Antoninus in the middle of a circle of Roman soldiers); Single Light Source (In his cell, Spartacus has only light come in from above); Reverse Tracking (When Batiatus is walking in the Libyan mines. When Spartacus is reviewing the former slaves the night before the big attack. When Varinia is walking towards the crucified Spartacus with their baby in her arms).

Audio Ideas: Voice-over (At the beginning); Dancing (The ex-slaves are shown enjoying themselves and loving life, but the Romans are not); Drums (Like the execution scene in *Paths Of Glory*, the big battle scene in *Spartacus* is set up with the use of drums. Kubrick cut to the exact drum beats which gives a chilling and memorable effect).

Themes: Hand-To-Hand (Lots of training, fighting in ring, on battle-field etc.); Nice To Animals (During Antoninus' act, little birds come out of eggs. When the gladiators escape, they force some Romans to fight in the gladiatorial arena but Spartacus is repulsed by this and stops them, asking: "Are we animals?" This echoes Saint-Auban's line about herd instinct in *Paths Of Glory*); The Beast In Man (At the revolt, Spart-acus is hunched over, holding a stick like the ape in *2001*); Staring/Eyes (Batiatus tells Marcellus to "keep an eye on Spartacus." Marcellus tells Spartacus: "Everything you do I'll be watching." Spartacus does a lot of staring. After the big battle many of the dead have their eyes open); Theatre (The fights to the death at Batiatus' gladiator school); Games (The Senate floor is chequered like a chessboard. The Romans play a board game in the sauna); Masks/Disguise (Crassus does not know what Spartacus looks like); Artificial Bodies (The gladiators are taught a series of stiff movements like machines, which they constantly repeat); The Collapse Of Society (With the slaves revolting, Rome is left without a financial base upon which to rely, and food and drink are running out. This is contrasted to the slaves who have water, wine, cows etc. upon which to live); Sexual Relations (Crassus is in love with Rome - he talks of not entering her with his army because that would violate her laws. He is in love with Varinia, whom he buys but never possesses - worse, she loves his enemy and has a child by him. He also desires Antoninus, who loves Spartacus and is willing to die for him. In the end Crassus gets Rome. He also gets Julius Caesar - in a persuasive argument half-naked in a sauna - whom he lures away from Gracchus).

Subtext: This film is obviously a left-wing comment on the power of the masses. The physical aspect of this is shown by Spartacus leading the revolt - the right of all men to be free to decide their future. The political aspect is shown in the debates and manoeuvres of Crassus and Gracchus in the Senate. Crassus believes he, as part of the elite, knows what is best for everybody, and wants to force everybody to do as he does, under the guise of patriotism. Gracchus is a republican, and believes in democracy, but also sees that the slaves are dangerous because they are changing the world too quickly, with no idea of how to control society once the change has been effected. The end, which shows both Spartacus and Gracchus dead, and the dictator Crassus controlling society, is rather simplistic. This can obviously be read as an allegory for the oppression of Senator McCarthy and the House Un-American Activities Committee, who hunted down Communists in the 1950s. A more interesting subtext is the sexual practices of the bisexual Crassus.

Background: When Kirk Douglas acquired the rights to Howard Fast's novel *Spartacus*, Fast insisted on writing the film script. It quickly became apparent that Fast's script would not do, so Douglas secretly hired screenwriter Dalton Trumbo to do the job - HUAC had sent Trumbo to jail for one year, he had been on the blacklist for ten years, and bizarrely he had won an Oscar for *The Brave One* in 1956 using a pseudonym. For *Spartacus*, Trumbo used the name Sam Jackson.

The race was on with *The Gladiators*, a rival production with the same subject matter, based on the novel by Arthur Koestler, directed by

Martin Ritt, starring Yul Brynner, scripted by Ira Wolfert (i.e. black-listed Abraham Polonsky who had written *Body And Soul* (1947, director Robert Rossen) and directed *Force Of Evil* (1948)). It was suggested at one time that both productions combine resources, but it never happened.

Universal Studios insisted that Anthony Mann, an experienced man, be brought in to direct *Spartacus*. On 27 January 1959, shooting began in Death Valley, which was the location for the opening scene at the Libyan mine. Mann handled it all okay and the footage he shot is all in the final edit. However, the following week, shooting the gladiator school in the back lot, Peter Ustinov was controlling Mann, directing his own scenes, and Douglas wasn't happy. Douglas, as co-producer of the film with his Bryna Productions, fired Mann on Friday 13 February and phoned Kubrick, who had to come up to speed over the weekend to start filming on the Monday.

Kubrick did not fit in. He did not have the respect of the veterans and did not attempt to socialise. Famously, he had a lot of arguments with cinematographer Russell Metty, who won an Oscar for the film. For one scene in a tent, Metty spent a long time setting up the lighting, when Kubrick walked in and said there was not enough light. Metty swore and angrily kicked a light onto the set. It slid to the feet of the actors and Kubrick said, "Now there is too much." Kubrick never got angry. The only time Kubrick seemed to open up was when editing - he would play baseball, joke.

The filming was not an ideal situation for Kubrick - he could not change the script but Trumbo was constantly rewriting the script, which meant that day-to-day Kubrick did not know what he was going to film. This generated a new working method - Kubrick had to think about the scene on set and he learnt to experiment and react to the actors on set rather than to totally lock everything down at the script stage. If there was no dialogue for a scene then Kubrick played mood music, just like in the silent days, to convey the emotion of a scene. This worked to great effect, especially in the scene where Spartacus and Draba wait to go into the arena to fight. Kubrick played a Prokofiev concerto on the close-up on Woody Strode as Draba.

Saul Bass had been brought in to design the titles - which are among the most brilliant he ever did - but he also contributed to the overall look and feel of the film. He found locations, like Death Valley for the opening scene, designed the gladiator school, did storyboards for the escape from the school (and came up with the idea of using the fallen fence as a weapon) and, most importantly, storyboarded the checkerboard layout of the advancing Roman legions for the final battle. Bass also came up with the idea for rolling logs on fire - a big hit with audiences but not historically accurate.

Virtually all the film was shot on the Universal Studios backlot - now the studio tour - with some locations in Death Valley, by the sea and in Spain. Total filming days: 167.

The movie was edited together and it was a disaster. Dalton Trumbo wrote an 80-page critique of the movie which Douglas described as "brilliant" in its understanding. Douglas got more budget so that the film could be reshot and restructured. Kubrick went to Spain for big shots of the masses marching across the landscape and for documentary inserts of slave camp life.

Douglas decided that Dalton Trumbo would be credited as the writer, thus breaking the blacklist. When the final edit of *Spartacus* was premièred, there were many nasty comments about a Commie writing a film from a book by a Commie. They obviously didn't know about the blacklisted actor, Peter Brocco, who played a supporting role. The situation was getting out of hand. Unusually, President John F Kennedy Jr. broke protocol to visit a Washington DC cinema to see *Spartacus* and gave it a good review.

Several scenes were cut due to protests from the Legion Of Decency including shots of men being dismembered. Seven years later, when the Oscar-winning film was reissued, an additional 22 minutes were chopped out. The Production Code Administration and the Legion of Decency both objected to the scene where Crassus attempts to seduce Antoninus in the bath, so it was cut. The 'lost' scenes were edited back into the restored version in 1991, but since the voicetrack to the seduction scene had been lost, Tony Curtis and Anthony Hopkins (Olivier had died) dubbed the dialogue.

Spot This: The great thing about historical epics is that you can watch the extras and background to find anachronisms. In *Spartacus*, a truck can be seen in the hills during a battle scene, and slave extras are quite happy to be seen wearing wristwatches and sandshoes.

The Verdict: Although Spartacus appears in most of the film, it is Crassus who is the most interesting character by far. Like George Macready's performance as Mireau in *Paths Of Glory*, Laurence Olivier's Crassus almost steals the show, although he has stiff competition from Charles Laughton and Peter Ustinov - the latter won the Oscar for Best Supporting Actor. This is an enjoyable historical romp, visually stunning, with complex characters and intelligent dialogue, but it rings false as a Kubrick film. The first half, with male bonding and military training, is brilliantly observed and tense. From then on, the power struggle in Rome takes our interest (à la Mireau and Broulard in *Paths Of Glory*), making Spartacus' story of freedom and domesticity seem trite and over-sentimental in comparison. In the end, it's a sad reflection on the film that Gracchus' suicide and Antoninus' tragic death are more affecting than Spartacus' crucifixion. 4/5

4: Eyesight

If *Spartacus* taught Kubrick one thing, it was that without control, he had nothing. Kubrick decided to change that situation. He would find a way to control script, cast, production, direction - everything. But what story could he use as a stepping stone?

While making *Spartacus*, both Kubrick and Harris found out about a new book called *Lolita* by Vladimir Nabokov. When they received a copy in the office, they were so excited to read it that Harris cracked the hardback spine and, as he read a page, would rip it out and hand it to Kubrick. When they finished, they knew they had to make it into a movie.

Lolita (1962)

Cast: James Mason (Humbert Humbert), Shelley Winters (Charlotte Haze), Sue Lyon (Lolita Haze), Peter Sellers (Clare Quilty), Garry Cockrell (Dick Schiller), Jerry Stovin (John Farlow), Diana Decker (Jean Farlow), Lois Maxwell (Nurse Lore)

Crew: Director Stanley Kubrick, Writers Vladimir Nabokov & Stanley Kubrick (uncredited), Novel Vladimir Nabokov, Producer James B Harris, Music Nelson Riddle, Lolita Theme Bob Harris, Orchestration Gil Grau, Cinematographer Oswald Morris, Editor Anthony Harvey, Art Director William C Andrews, 152 minutes

Story: A foggy forest. We move forward, following a car to a big house. Humbert Humbert enters the house and prowls around it, eventually meeting Clare Quilty, drunk, in a sheet ("I'm Spartacus. Have you come to free the slaves or something?"). Quilty plays table tennis. When Humbert pulls a gun, Quilty calls him a bad loser. Humbert hands Quilty a note, the reason why, written like bad poetry, which Quilty critiques. Quilty puts on boxing gloves and runs when Humbert shoots. Humbert empties the gun, hitting Quilty's leg. Quilty crawls up the stairs and hides behind a painting of an elegant young lady as Humbert walks up the stairs reloading his gun. Humbert puts bullets through the painting, and Quilty dies.

4 years earlier, Humbert arrives in West Ramsdale, looking for lodgings for the summer. He's a part-time poet and full-time Professor - he will be teaching the French romantics at Beardsley College. Charlotte

Haze shows Humbert around her house, flirting with him, but he's obviously not interested in her or the house. Then, as Charlotte says "my cherry pie," he sees Lolita. Cut to a scream, a film monster staring at us, and Lolita, Humbert and Charlotte in a car watching *The Mummy*. As the women scream, they put their hands on Humbert's knees, Humbert takes his hand away from Charlotte's and puts it on Lolita's. As Charlotte and Humbert play chess, with Lolita looking on, Charlotte says, "You're going to take my queen." "That's my intention," replies Humbert, who then wins the match.

At the school dance, they meet John and Jean Farlow, who confess to being broad-minded (hinting that they would like a sexual foursome with Humbert & Charlotte). Clare Quilty, TV writer, who once gave a talk on Dr Schweitzer and Dr Zhivago, is at the dance - Charlotte had a fling with him. Humbert is too engrossed with Lolita dancing with a boyfriend to notice that it is arranged for him and Charlotte to be alone that night.

Back at the house, Charlotte tries to seduce Humbert but Lolita comes home just as Charlotte is kissing Humbert and spoils it all. From then on, Charlotte is annoyed with Lolita. Lolita and Humbert have their first meeting - he reads her poetry by Edgar Allan Poe, and she feeds him fish. Charlotte arranges for Lolita to go off to summer camp. Lolita kisses Humbert as she leaves and says, "Don't forget me." Realising that he will never see her again, since he is only there for the summer, Humbert lies in her room depressed. He opens a letter from Charlotte, in which she proposes love and marriage, to which Humbert's reply is to laugh loud and long. They marry.

Humbert spends a lot of time in the bathroom, writing his diary and trying to escape from Charlotte. He considers making love to her a sacrifice and she wants to make love often. She is forever bossing him around. "Every game has its rules," he says, and she's going too far. Humbert considers murdering her with her gun and plans the perfect murder, but chickens out. He discovers Charlotte reading his diary, in which he calls her a cow and other things. He goes downstairs to make her a drink, then gets a telephone call saying his wife has been in a car accident. He runs outside, into the rain, and Charlotte is dead.

Humbert is happy, but drunk, in the bath. The Farlows come to visit and, seeing the gun, think Humbert is contemplating suicide. They tell him he has to live for Lolita now…

At Camp Climax, Humbert meets Charlie, the only boy at the girls' camp, and then picks up Lolita. He tells her that her mother is ill and he is driving her to the hospital. Humbert: "What makes you say I've stopped caring for you?" Lolita: "Well, you haven't even kissed me yet, have you?" The car roars away to the hotel.

At the hotel, the night manager Mr Swine, says that they only have one room with one bed. Humbert is embarrassed because of this, and also because of the police convention at the hotel. Quilty is there and overhears what is going on. To capitalise on Humbert's embarrassment, Quilty pretends to be a policeman and, in his conversation, there are many jabs and jokes at Humbert's expense, especially an overuse of the word 'normal.' Humbert arranges for a cot, and spends the night in it at the foot of the bed. When he wakes, Lolita asks if he wants to play a game, one she played with Charlie at Camp Climax. At last, Humbert makes love to Lolita.

On the road, Humbert tells Lolita that her mother is dead. Lolita laughs, then cries in the motel. "Promise you'll never leave me," she pleas. Humbert holds her in his arms.

Later, Humbert is teaching at Beardsley College and Lolita is going to school. Humbert is jealous of her being in contact with boys, watching her every move, every word, looking for things to be wrong. They argue constantly. Lolita is acting in a play and says she wants him to be proud of her. Humbert forbids her to be in it. That night the German Dr Zemsh, the school psychologist, visits Humbert and threatens to bring Dr Cuddler and his team to the house to work out the source of repression in Lolita's libido - to prevent this happening Humbert agrees for Lolita to be in the play. Lolita is a great success in the school play, written by Clare Quilty among others.

When Humbert discovers Lolita had not been to her piano lessons he wonders where she had gone. Jealous, angry, they have a fight and Lolita walks out. After Lolita makes a phone call, she goes back to Humbert and they go on the road again. Soon, Humbert realises they are being followed and, when Lolita becomes ill, he takes her to hospital. After he receives a threatening phone call, he finds her gone from the hospital - Humbert goes wild with panic and is treated like a mental patient by the staff. An Uncle has taken Lolita - she has disappeared.

Three years later Mrs Richard T Schiller, as Lolita is now known, writes to Humbert and asks for money. Humbert arrives, still in love, still believing that he can whisk her away, but it soon becomes apparent his dream is not to be. Lolita is older, pregnant, married to a low-income labourer with a hearing aid. They plan to go to Alaska. Lolita tells Humbert what really happened, that she had been in love with Quilty all along, that he had been her lover, that he was Dr Zemsh, the policeman at the hotel, the man who followed them in the car and the mysterious phone caller. "He was the only guy I was ever really crazy about." After running away from Humbert, Quilty had tried to make Lolita do things she didn't like, like appearing in 'art' movies. She eventually left him. Whilst crying, Humbert hands over $13,000 in money and deeds.

Humbert makes his way to Quilty's house and shoots him. Before his case comes to trial, Humbert dies of a heart attack.

Visual Ideas: Corridors (At the hospital when Humbert is being escorted out by two men it is like the two men in *Killer's Kiss* and *The Killing*); Film Noir/Expressionism (Being followed by the car. In the hotel, the layers of light make the bedroom look like a cage); Reverse Tracking (When Humbert goes to kill Charlotte); Signs (Camp Climax for girls. Mr Swine the hotel manager. Dr Cuddler the child psychologist. Miss Fromkiss the nurse. Nurse Lore. Dr Keygee); Colour Coding (Lolita is in white or light colours. Humbert is in light colours at the beginning, but after he makes love to Lolita he is in black).

Audio Ideas: Voice-over (Humbert is heard repeatedly throughout the movie); The Waltz/Dancing (The school dance. Charlotte dances for Humbert); Ironic Music (Throughout the film the music acts as a counterpoint to the psychological state of the characters. For example, after Charlotte dies, we hear cheerful music whilst Humbert is in the bath); Sound (To punctuate an idea, Kubrick uses loud sound. For example, when Humbert collects Lolita from the summer camp, she complains he hasn't even kissed her yet, which cuts to a very large roar from the car).

Themes: Hand-To-Hand (The fight in the hospital); Nice To Animals (Richard T Schiller is crazy about dogs and kids); Staring/Eyes (In the garden, Lolita stares at Humbert); Theatre (Drive-in film. Lolita in the school play); Games (Table tennis, boxing, chess, hula hoop); Masks/Disguise (Lolita makes a face at her mother. Lolita in make-up for the play. Quilty as the policeman & Dr Zemsh); Technology (Cot beds are seriously complicated pieces of apparatus); The Fatal Flaw (Humbert's love for Lolita destroys him); The Paralysed Man/Illness (Quilty is shot in the leg. Richard T Schiller has a hearing aid); The Collapse Of Society (Kubrick shows a hypocritical society which indulges in wife-swapping and other sexual activities); Family Relationships (Charlotte wants to be sexually active and is jealous of her more attractive daughter. Humbert wants to be Lolita's 'husband' but has to settle for father - Freud would have loved this. Lolita is quite happy to follow her mother's example and jump into bed with whomsoever she desires. The triangle is perfectly explained when Humbert embraces Charlotte and looks at a photo of Lolita - Lolita looks back impassively).

Subtext: Like *Spartacus* and *Killer's Kiss*, this is about two men who want one woman. Both Humbert and Quilty slept with Charlotte to get to Lolita. Quilty has no inhibitions about the things he does and he has probably explored every vice there is - attend executions, make 'art' movies, drink, sex etc. He is a vulgar version of what Humbert wants to be. Humbert wants to be free to love Lolita rather than just have sex with her. When Humbert hunts down and kills Quilty, he is not only killing the man who 'stole' his girl, but the vulgarity of sex with Lolita. He is also punishing the dark side of himself. In the novel, Humbert is sexually obsessed with the form of Lolita and it is only at the end that we learn that he truly loves her.

Background: To get $150,000 for the film rights to *Lolita*, Harris and Kubrick had to sell all their rights to *The Killing* to United Artists. They also bought the rights to Nabokov's *Laughter In The Dark*, which had a similar theme, to protect their investment. It was a good investment. After a year in the best-seller charts, *Lolita* had sold almost 300,000 copies, and would go on to sell more than 14 million copies worldwide.

Who was to write the screenplay? Nabokov refused, and Calder Willingham's attempt was rejected by Kubrick. The problem was how to get the subject matter through the conservative censorship system. The film had been nagging in Nabokov's mind, and he had come up with some ideas, so he agreed to write the screenplay. Moving to Hollywood, he wrote two drafts of the screenplay from March to September 1960, incorporating ideas and scenes he had not included in the novel. Although he would receive full writing credit, Kubrick and Harris rewrote and edited it to get it past the censors.

Who would be Lolita? Early on, Kubrick found Tuesday Weld, but she was not considered suitable by Nabokov. After many mothers put forward their daughters (and sometimes themselves), Kubrick settled on 14-year-old Sue Lyon, whom he had seen on an episode of *The Loretta Young Show*. She was to play Lolita, who would age from 12 to 17 over the course of the film.

Who would be Humbert Humbert? James Mason was Kubrick's first choice but he had to decline because of a stage role. Laurence Olivier, David Niven and even Marlon Brando all said yes, but their agents did not want their talent associated with the subject. Then, as luck would have it, all Mason's friends said he should play the role, and Mason was a great admirer of Nabokov, so he was in.

Where to shoot it? Harris-Kubrick had $1 million to play with, so they decided to play in England, where the Eady plan allowed film-makers to write off costs if 80% of the labour were English.

Before shooting began, Kubrick gave the actors a generous amount of time to learn their lines, then forget them and improvise them - the improvised version being the one they stuck to on set. The only exception to this rule was Peter Sellers, whom Kubrick encouraged to improvise on set, starting with the lines as written, and then going off in all directions. When Kubrick found what he wanted, Sellers would repeat the routine for one take, three or more cameras on him. Kubrick was keen that Nabokov a) not find out Kubrick had rewritten the script and b) not learn that the actors had rewritten his lines.

The film was shot in 88 days at a cost of just over $2 million. It was then edited to comply with the 'suggestions' of the censoring bodies (the main one being fading out quicker when Lolita suggests to Humbert that they play a game). *Lolita* was condemned by the Legion of Decency, which basically meant that every Catholic in the country was told not to see it - watching *Lolita* was a mortal sin. This is obviously the reason it took $4.5 million on its opening run.

The Verdict: It is a daring picture in terms of subject matter, but the problem is with the structure. In the first third we see Humbert as a knowing person - he is in control and it is fun watching him critique small-town America. In the second third, Humbert makes a commitment to Lolita, and does this by marrying her mother and then, when Charlotte dies, taking Lolita across America. From this moment, Humbert loses his dignity, and Lolita's motives are never clearly explained. In the final third, when domestic life with Lolita fails, and Humbert makes a run for it with her, there is too much mystery (Lolita's motive? Who is following them?) and not enough resolution to sufficiently hold our interest. Peter Sellers is slightly too zany. Sue Lyon is too bland. Shelley Winters is just right. James Mason is great considering he's playing a paedophile. 3/5

Dr Strangelove
Or: How I Learned To Stop Worrying And Love The Bomb (1964)

Cast: Peter Sellers (Group Captain Lionel Mandrake/President Merkin Muffley/Dr Strangelove), George C Scott (General 'Buck' Turgidson), Sterling Hayden (General Jack D Ripper), Keenan Wynn (Colonel 'Bat' Guano), Slim Pickens (Major T J 'King' Kong), Peter Bull (Ambassador de Sadesky), James Earl Jones (Lieutenant Lothar Zogg)

Crew: Director & Producer Stanley Kubrick, Writers Stanley Kubrick & Terry Southern & Peter George, Novel *Red Alert* aka *Two Hours To Doom* Peter George, Associate Producer Victor Lyndon, Executive Producer Leon Minoff, Music Laurie Johnson, Cinematographer Gilbert Taylor, Editor Anthony Harvey, Production Design Ken Adam, Special Effects Advisor Arthur 'Weegee' Fellig (uncredited), Technical Advisor Captain John Crewdson, Title Designer Pablo Ferro, 93 minutes

Story: American bombers constantly fly around the Soviet borders waiting for the orders to drop their load on designated targets.

Burpelson Air Force Base: General Jack D Ripper tells Group Captain Lionel Mandrake (on loan from the RAF) that the Soviets have attacked Washington and that they are to go to Red Alert.

On board one of the B-52s, Major Kong and his men are relaxing, reading *Playboy* and paperbacks, or doing card tricks when they receive a coded message on the CRM 114. The message is 'Wing Attack Plan R.'

Pentagon: General 'Buck' Turgidson's affair with his secretary is interrupted by a telephone call saying that the bombs are in the air, and no outside lines are connected to General Ripper.

B-52: Major Kong, now wearing his cowboy hat, issues the papers for Plan R to his crew and they go through the procedure. This includes setting the CRM 114 so that it only receives messages with the prefix OPE. Their primary target is Laputa.

Burpelson: Ripper ordered Mandrake to collect all radios on Burpelson Air Force Base, but Mandrake notices that all the civilian stations are still operating so no bombs have been dropped. When he goes to tell this news to Ripper, he's locked in by Ripper, who explains that he's forcing a war so that America will win. According to Ripper, the Commies have been sapping and impurifying the precious bodily fluids of Americans.

War Room: President Merkin Muffley, General Turgidson and the joint chiefs of staff meet to discuss the situation. Turgidson fills them in, pointing out that Plan R was conceived to allow lower ranks to activate the bomb in retaliation, just in case the ruling powers were unable to do so. Unfortunately, some human error crept in.

B-52: The bomber crew check their survival kit, which includes lipsticks, nylons and a prophylactic.

War Room: The Russian Ambassador de Sadesky enters the War Room and is shown around the food table. Turgidson and de Sadesky fight and the President shouts at them, "Gentlemen. You can't fight in here - this is the War Room!" On the phone to Premier Dimitri Kissov, the President tells Dimitri that it's a "friendly call," and that the US want to help the Russians destroy the planes. "Who should we call?" the President asks. Kissov tells him but doesn't have their number, so recommends the President call Omsk directory enquiries. Kissov tells his Ambassador about the Doomsday Machine they have just developed which, upon nuclear attack, releases a radiation shroud over the Earth and kills all human and animal life. Dr Strangelove explains how such a machine would work but says that it only works as a deterrent if everybody else knows about it. The Ambassador says that the Premier wanted to announce it at the Party Conference on Monday, "The Premier loves surprises."

Burpelson: Ripper explains to Mandrake that water is the source of all life, but he only drinks distilled water or rainwater because of fluoridation - a monstrous Commie plot begun in 1946. Ripper first started to notice a great emptiness after he had given his life essence during the act of making love. Since then, he has never given a woman his life essence. Ripper's troops surrender and Ripper begins to worry about the torture he'll be subjected to to get the code - he shoots himself.

B-52: A missile is after the plane and the chase is on. They evade it, only for the detonation to damage the plane.

Burpelson: Mandrake looks at Ripper's doodles and sees the phrase Peace On Earth repeated time after time. He also remembers Ripper's phrase 'Purity Of Essence.' Colonel 'Bat' Guano enters and takes Mandrake prisoner.

B-52: The CRM 114 is destroyed, which means they cannot receive messages. Major Kong flies under the radar to avoid detection.

Burpelson: Guano thinks Mandrake is some sort of PRE-vert, subject to many PRE-versions. Mandrake convinces him that he has to make a call to the President, but the phone lines are cut, so he tries the pay-phone. He tries to put a collect call through to the President but Mandrake is 20 cents short, so Guano shoots open the Coca-Cola machine for change.

War Room: The OPE code is found and all the planes are recalled, but one plane is missing.

B-52: Running out of fuel, Kong changes target and goes through the procedure for the final bombing run. The bomb doors won't open, so Kong goes down to open them manually. He sits on one of the bombs, opens the door, the bomb is released and Kong goes down with the bomb, riding it like a bucking bronco. Silence. The bomb explodes.

War Room: The Doomsday Machine will be triggered, so Dr Strangelove suggests that a few people should be selected to go down the deepest mine shafts for 100 years. They should be selected because of intelligence, and of course they will have to breed, so there will be 10 women for every man. They are all men, so they like the idea.

Bombs: Lots of nuclear devices explode to the sound of Vera Lynn singing 'We'll Meet Again.'

Visual Ideas: Mirrors (General Turgidson's room is walled with mirrors so that he can see himself and his secretary); Symmetry (The War Room is symmetrical); Film Noir/Expressionism (The harsh light in the War Room and Ripper's office. When Dr Strangelove is in the dark and only the rim of his glasses shine); Hand-Held (The attack on Burpelson Air Force Base looks like documentary footage. Also on board the bomber, the hand-held camera makes everything seem fast and distorted. All the hand-held camerawork was done by Kubrick himself); Circles (The table in the War Room is a circle); Single Light Source (There are single lights above General Ripper's desk and above the War Room table); Reverse Tracking (The B-52 is seen coming towards us); Signs (In Burpelson one sign reads, 'Peace Is Our Profession,' and during the fighting the soldiers ignore the 'Keep Off The Grass' sign. In the War Room, one of the folders is entitled, 'World Targets In Megadeaths.' The bombs are labelled 'Hi There!' and 'Dear John.' In the novel, the latter was labelled 'Lolita').

Audio Ideas: Voice-over (A couple of times at the beginning); Ironic Music (The opening music is 'Try A Little Tenderness.' For the bomber, the western music 'When Johnny Comes Marching Home' is used - usually heard in John Ford westerns for the cavalry. At the end, the destruction of the world isn't the end because 'We'll Meet Again').

Themes: Hand-To-Hand (Turgidson and the Russian Ambassador fight); Staring/Eyes (General Ripper stares); Theatre (Theatre of war?); Games (Cards); Masks/Disguise (Turgidson, Strangelove, Kong, Ripper and the Russian Ambassador all have exaggerated faces); Technology (Computers, CRM 114 code machine, nuclear bombs, radar and spy cameras); The Fatal Flaw (Human error); The Paralysed Man/Illness (Dr Strangelove is in a wheelchair and has an arm with a will of its own. General Ripper is mad); The Collapse Of Society (This society is destroyed so the people who destroyed it immediately come up with another society (in mine shafts) that will inevitably fail); Family Relationships (Nobody mentions or thinks of family).

Subtext: As in *Paths Of Glory*, Kubrick shows how a male society gets beyond the control of man. General Ripper, like General Mireau, has gone a little mad and unleashed something his colleagues cannot stop. The story takes place in three locations: the château/war room; the trenches/Burpelson; no man's land/B-52. At the end, after failing to avert the crisis (three men shot/end of the world), the men return to their normal routine none the wiser. In *Dr Strangelove*, that means that the Ambassador continues spying, and General Turgidson continues worrying about keeping up with the Soviets etc. Man may change the world around him, but man himself does not change.

There are other allegories available, the foremost of which is sex: the phallic coupling of the planes refuelling with the music 'Try A Little Tenderness'; Jack D Ripper (19th-century sex criminal) will not give up his bodily fluids but initiates Attack Plan R - R for Romeo; Ripper carries many phallic symbols (gun in waistband, big gun in golf bag and an enormous cigar) and eventually kills himself with one of them; Buck Turgidson (meaning 'male' or 'swollen') mixes weapons and sex when he talks to his secretary, wanting her to "start her countdown" so that she'll be ready for 'blast-off'; President Merkin Muffley (both names are references to female pudendum); on the B-52, the two bombs have writing on them - 'Dear John' is the start of a letter breaking off an affair - and Major Kong unforgettably rides one of the phallic bombs to its climax; finally the joy of sex, of strange love, the beautiful nuclear mushrooms/phallus. In Jonathan Swift's 1726 novel *Gulliver's Travels*, Laputa is a place inhabited by caricatures of scientific researchers - it also mean whore in Spanish and Italian.

Background: Kubrick was afraid of a nuclear bomb dropping on him. Since the subject was of some interest to him, when he found out about *Red Alert* by Peter George (originally published as *Two Hours To Doom* under the pseudonym Peter Bryant), Kubrick purchased the film rights and worked with George to generate a screenplay. As usual, Kubrick devoured all the standard texts on the subject by the people who made the bomb, the people who decide where to drop it, as well as the philosophers considering whether or not we should have it in the first place. However, playing around with Harris late one night, they started making fun of the situation, adding inappropriate ideas. Nothing happened that night, but later Kubrick decided that a nightmare comedy would be the best way to approach the subject, and brought in novelist/screenwriter Terry Southern to do the dreaming.

Meanwhile, after ten years of working together, James B Harris decided to leave the team to start a directing career. The break-up was amicable, and it gave Kubrick the opportunity to totally control every aspect of his work.

Because of costs, Kubrick made the film in Shepperton Studios in England. Each morning at 5 a.m. Terry Southern would meet Kubrick at his house in Knightsbridge and spend two hours in the back of Kubrick's old Bentley adding new ideas to the script on the way to the studios.

Originally, Peter Sellers was cast in four roles, but couldn't find the right Texan accent for Major 'King' Kong. Fortunately for Sellers, he 'hurt' his ankle, so on the advice of designer Ken Adam, Kubrick brought in Slim Pickens, a former rodeo clown and rider who had been in *One-Eyed Jacks*. Pickens was never shown the script nor was he told it was a black comedy; but was ordered by Kubrick to play it straight, which he did.

Sellers based Dr Strangelove's strangled accent on the voice of Weegee, the famous German-born crime photographer of the 1950s whose name was given to him by the New York police due to his uncanny ability to show up at murder scenes before they did (i.e. as though he owned a Ouija board). When Weegee, real name Arthur Fellig, visited the set, Sellers heard him talking and adopted his strange German accent.

As the production continued, news came in that a similar film was being made based on *Fail-Safe*, a novel by Eugene Burdick and Harvey Wheeler. The idea was that it would be filmed and released before *Dr Strangelove*. Afraid of the effect it might have on grosses, Kubrick sued for plagiarism. Eventually, Columbia Pictures bought both films for distribution and released *Fail-Safe* (1964, director Sidney Lumet) 10 months after *Dr Strangelove*.

The film was to end with a custard pie fight between the Russians and the Americans in the War Room (which is why we see a big table of food there). The footage was shot, but Kubrick decided not to use it because he considered it too farcical to fit in with the dark satire of the rest of the film. At one point, President Muffley takes a pie in the face and falls down, prompting Turgidson to cry, "Gentlemen! Our gallant young president has just been struck down in his prime!" As it happened, President Kennedy was assassinated in Dallas on the day of the press launch, which was cancelled out of respect. This also necessitated a line change. Major Kong's comment about the survival kit ("A fella could have a pretty good weekend in Vegas with all that stuff,") originally referred to Dallas instead of Las Vegas, but was overdubbed after the assassination.

The Verdict: Like *Lolita*, this is a black comedy. Unlike *Lolita*, *Dr Strangelove* is handled perfectly. There is complete detachment from the characters, yet at the same time there is total involvement in the story. Every laugh has a barb behind it. Erudite. Intelligent. Visually stunning. Masterpiece. 5/5

2001: A Space Odyssey (1968)

Cast: Keir Dullea (David Bowman), Gary Lockwood (Frank Poole), William Sylvester (Dr Heywood R Floyd), Daniel Richter (Moonwatcher), Leonard Rossiter (Smyslov), Margaret Tyzack (Elena), Robert Beatty (Dr Halvorsen), Sean Sullivan (Michaels), Douglas Rain (voice of HAL 9000), Ed Bishop (Lunar Shuttle Captain), Vivian Kubrick (Squirt), Anya & Katharina Kubrick (Painting Girls in deleted scenes)

Crew: Director & Producer Stanley Kubrick, Writers Stanley Kubrick & Arthur C Clarke, Story 'The Sentinel' Arthur C Clarke, Music Aram Khachaturyan (from 'Ballet Suite Gayaneh') György Ligeti (from 'Atmospheres,' 'Lux Aeterna,' 'Adventures' and 'Requiem') Richard Strauss (from 'Also Sprach Zarathustra') Johann Strauss (from 'Blue

Danube Waltz'), Cinematographer John Alcott, Additional Photography Geoffrey Unsworth, Editor Ray Lovejoy, Production Design Ernest Archer & Harry Lange & Anthony Masters, Special Photographic Effects Supervisors Stanley Kubrick & Douglas Trumbull & Wally Veevers, 156 minutes for the première, 139 minutes for general release. Germany 133 minutes

Working Title: Journey Beyond The Stars (1965)

Story: Apes gather for food and water, and sleep together. They eat roots with the other animals. They are forced away from their watering hole by other apes so they find it difficult to survive. The monolith appears. One ape finds out how to use bones as tools/weapons. The apes learn to hunt and eat the animals they once ate beside. The apes take back the watering hole from their rivals, and beat one of them to death. In triumph, an ape throws the bone into the air.

Next we are in a future society and we watch people eat and drink on spaceships - they are carrying their air, water and food around with them into the vacuum of space. In this case, the enemy is the Russian sector. The monolith appears on the Moon, and the Americans and Russians co-operate by throwing an even bigger stick into space - Discovery 1 - on a manned mission to Jupiter. We watch Bowman and Poole eat, drink, play chess, draw. Their enemy is HAL who kills Poole and throws Bowman off his 'watering hole.' Bowman removes HAL's intelligence (essentially destroys the head, like the ape bashed in the head of the enemy ape). The monolith appears in space, and Bowman goes through the star gate, witnessing the wonders of the universe. In a familiar setting, an 18th-century suite, he ages and transforms physically into a star child, then returns to Earth carrying his own environment with him - his womb.

Visual Ideas: Mirrors (In the 18th century bathroom, Bowman looks in the mirror and sees that he is old); Corridors (Going through the star gate); Symmetry (The film is littered with symmetry); Expressionism (When Bowman is going through the star gate, we see still pictures of his head in contortions); Hand-Held (When the astronauts are walking down into the monolith pit on the Moon, and when Bowman breaks back into Discovery to kill HAL); Circles (Planets, moons, the space station is like a wheel, the shuttle to the Moon, the pods on the Discovery); Single Light Source (In the 18th-century suite the light source is from the floor); Reverse Tracking (When Bowman is running around the main deck of the Discovery); Red (The colour of death, danger and birth. Red is seen at the dawn of man sunrise, the red meat, the red cockpits of all the spaceships, the red mind of HAL and the red suit Bowman wears); CRM 114 (The code box from *Dr Strangelove* is now the designated serial number of Discovery 1).

Audio Ideas: Titles ('Also Sprach Zarathustra' by Richard Strauss is used in one of the most famous title sequences of all time. The cuts are synchronised exactly with the music); The Waltz ('The Blue Danube' is used when the shuttle is going to the space station, and then on the journey to the Moon); Breathing (When Poole and Bowman go outside Discovery all we can hear is their rapid breathing); Beeps (Everything in the future has its own sound. The beeps and buzzes of technology create their own soundtrack for the film).

Themes: Hand-To-Hand (The apes fight. HAL makes the pod hit Poole); Nice To Animals (Floyd's daughter wants a bush baby); Staring/ Eyes (The ape stares at the Moon. HAL is an always-staring red eye. Bowman stares at the universe); Theatre (Floyd stands up in front of the staff on the Moon base to give a speech); Games (Poole plays chess with HAL); The 18th Century (The suite at the end); Bars (On the space station); Artificial Bodies (The crew in hibernation. The suits standing in the pod room); Technology (Zero gravity toilets. Food dispensers. Video phones. Interplanetary craft. Voice print identification); The Paralysed Man/Illness (The crew in hibernation. Bowman as an old man); Family Relationships (Dr Heywood Floyd talks to his daughter and sends his love to his wife. Frank Poole receives a birthday message from his parents); Birth (Bowman's rebirth is inevitable: the birthdays of Dr Floyd's child, HAL and Poole are mentioned, and it takes 9 months for Discovery 1 to reach Jupiter); Apollo (The 'bowman' of Greek mythology is Apollo, the god of prophecy. As a prophet and magician, he is the patron of medicine and healing. Apollo, of course, is also the name of the American manned space missions during the 1960s).

Subtext: In a word - evolution. And what's more, evolution triggered by an outside force. At each stage, man continues to kill and be killed. The question is, will this newest evolution be any different? Or will we still act like animals?

Background: Kubrick had been looking for a science fiction subject since 1957 and had been researching both science fiction and non-fiction for some considerable time. Through a friend, he contacted Arthur C Clarke, who suggested his story 'The Sentinel' would provide a suitable starting point - it deals with the discovery of a monolith on the Moon which is a marker placed there by aliens. Clarke had written the story for a BBC competition in 1948, but it didn't even make the shortlist.

Clarke wrote the novel of *2001* in the Chelsea Hotel (home to William S Burroughs and many other bohemian-beatnik authors) while Kubrick worked on the screenplay - they worked off each other's ideas to form a cohesive whole.

Martin Balsam and Nigel Davenport were both suggested for the voice of HAL 9000, but were too emotional for Kubrick's liking. Douglas Rain did the voice and never visited the set. Yes, I know that if you take the next letter of each letter of HAL, you get IBM. This is a complete fluke, and Kubrick and Clarke came up with the name from joining 'Heurisitic' and 'Algorithm' which is the way HAL was supposed to have learned everything. The song 'Daisy,' which HAL sings as he is being shut down, was the first song ever played by a non-mechanical computer. Appropriately, the lyrics include the phrase 'I'm half crazy.' When HAL and Poole play chess, the positions and moves we see are from a game played in 1913 in Hamburg between two players named Roesch and Schlage.

When Bowman re-enters the ship, he is exposed to vacuum for no more than 10 seconds before operating the repressurisation valve. People sometimes complain that this is not possible because they see heads and bodies explode in other movies, but scientific evidence shows that this would indeed be survivable without grievous harm.

The film originally premièred at 160 minutes. After that Kubrick removed about twenty minutes of scenes and made a few changes: Scenes of the apes, the monolith on the Moon, and the routine life of the astronauts aboard Discovery were removed. The titles 'Jupiter Mission, 18 Months Later' and 'Jupiter Beyond The Infinite' were added.

2001 won the Oscar for best Special Effects, the only Oscar Kubrick ever received.

Legacies: Arthur C Clarke has followed the original novel with *2010: Odyssey Two* and *2061: Odyssey Three*. Although intelligent, they do not have the mystical edge of *2001*. A film of *2010* was made in 1984, directed by Peter Hyams. Kubrick and Clarke cameo as the US and Russian leaders on the cover of *Time* magazine.

The Verdict: Although Kubrick retains some of his ideas and visual style from previous films, this is so different from what has gone before that it just takes your breath away. This is enchanting visual poetry. 5/5

5: The Stare

Having made his last three films in England, Kubrick made the decision to live there permanently - he moved his family into Abbott's Mead, a mansion in the Hertfordshire countryside. Over the years, journalists would assert that Kubrick was a hermit and 'awkward' and 'sinister' mainly because they were frustrated at Kubrick's reticence to play the media game. He did not concentrate on becoming famous but on making his films. However, although he was away from the public eye, he never cut himself off from his friends. He was constantly on the phone to people all over the world, irrespective of their time zones. The subject of his talk ranged from philosophical to political to sociological to scientific - often in the same conversation.

After finishing *2001*, Kubrick spent time developing a film on Napoleon, which basically required a country to hire out its armed forces for a period of time. Kubrick planned to film battle scenes with 35,000 people or more - they would make 4,000 costumes, then the rest would be throwaway overalls with the design painted on them. The battles would be recreated in full. Napoleon created modern Europe, and Kubrick thought the concerns of those times were contemporary - the responsibilities and abuses of power, the dynamics of social revolution, the relationship of the individual to the state, war, militarism etc. For the lead, Kubrick talked to a young actor by the name of Jack Nicholson. There were two problems: a) getting the finance, b) compressing the enormous amount of data Kubrick and his team had collated into a narrative form which made emotional sense. All that remains is the research and a script.

Meanwhile, Kubrick had moved onto another project, one involving ultra-violence and a debate about free will narrated by a thug.

A Clockwork Orange (1971)

Cast: Malcolm McDowell (Alex DeLarge), Patrick Magee (Frank Alexander), Michael Bates (Chief Guard Barnes), Warren Clarke (Dim), John Clive (Stage Actor), Adrienne Corri (Mrs Alexander), Carl Duering (Dr Brodsky), Paul Farrell (Tramp), Clive Francis (Lodger), Michael Gover (Prison Governor), Miriam Karlin (Cat Lady), James Marcus (Georgie), Aubrey Morris (PR Deltoid), Godfrey Quigley (Prison Chaplain), Sheila Raynor (Mrs DeLarge, M), Madge Ryan (Dr Branum), John Savident (Conspirator Dolin), Anthony Sharp (Minister), Philip Stone (Mr DeLarge, P), Pauline Taylor (Dr Taylor), Margaret Tyzack (Rubinstein), Steven Berkoff (Constable), Lindsay Campbell (Detective), Michael Tarn (Pete), David Prowse (Julian, Frank Alexander's Bodyguard, Therapist)

Crew: Director & Writer & Producer Stanley Kubrick, Novel Anthony Burgess, Executive Producers Si Litvinoff & Max L Raab, Associate Producer Bernard Williams, Music Walter Carlos, Cinematographer John Alcott, Editor William Butler, Production Design John Barry, Sculptures & Paintings Christiane Kubrick, 137 minutes

Story: Alex and his three droogs/friends have a drink of moloko/milk before going out on the town. They beat up a drunk, rumble a rival gang who are raping a woman, steal a car, drive like maniacs, attack writer Frank Alexander and force him to watch as Alex rapes his wife - Alex kicking, beating, raping while singing/dancing 'Singin' In The Rain' - before returning to the Korova milk bar. Returning home very late, Alex takes a piss, plays with Basil his pet snake and listens to Ludwig Van Beethoven's glorious *Ninth Symphony*, imagining war, explosions, vampires, hanging, death and destruction.

Next morning, Alex does not go to school - he's only 15 - so the Collector comes to visit and gives Alex due warning. Alex goes to the local record shop, picks up two girls, brings them home and fucks them. Georgie and Dim want more money, and Georgie takes over the group. Alex waits, then beats up Georgie and Dim, reasserting his leadership.

They go to a health farm, break in and Alex kills the cat-woman with a giant phallus. As he leaves, his droogs smash a bottle of moloko in his face, and leave him for the police.

Imprisoned for 14 years, Alex spends 2 years toadying to the prison chaplain. Reading *The Bible*, he re-enacts parts in his head - Alex as the

Roman guard whipping Jesus, fighting à la Spartacus, cavorting with naked hand maidens.

Trying to find a way out, Alex volunteers for the experimental Ludovico Treatment, which will cure him in two weeks, ready for release into society. The chaplain warns, "When a man cannot choose, he is no longer a man." In the clinic, Alex is given a drug (serum 114) then, in a cinema, he is bound to a chair, his eyes are clamped open and he is forced to watch films of violence and depravity whilst listening to Ludwig Van's glorious *Ninth Symphony*. After two weeks, the mere thought of sex, violence and the *Ninth* throws Alex into convulsions.

Alex is publicly tested in front of the press and government minister, then released into the world. His parents disown him and throw Alex out, having found a nice lodger. Old age pensioners assault him, but he is saved by two policemen - Georgie and Dim - who take him into the country and beat him up. Stumbling to the nearest house, Alex is helped by the writer whose wife he had raped, but is not recognised.

As Alex relaxes in the water, he starts humming 'Singin' In The Rain,' the writer remembers, becomes angry and then kidnaps Alex. Alex wakens in a room, listening to the glorious *Ninth*, becoming ill. He can't take it anymore, so he throws himself out of the window.

Waking in hospital covered in plaster casts, Alex's parents visit and are sorry for chucking him out. Also, the Government are in trouble because the Ludovico Treatment is being blamed for driving Alex to attempt suicide. Without Alex knowing, the doctors have been tinkering with his brain and have reversed the process. The Minister responsible offers Alex an interesting job with a good salary, shakes hands and they pose for the press. Alex listens to Ludwig Van's glorious *Ninth* and thinks of having sex with a woman. He is back the way he was.

Visual Ideas: Mirrors (The writer's house has a corridor of mirrors, and a mirror in the bathroom); Symmetry (The opening shot in the bar, the beating of the drunk, and lots more); Film Noir/Expressionism (Beating up the drunk); Hand-Held (When the droogs break into the writer's house and Alex's attack on the cat-woman); Circles (Alex's light in his room. The prisoners walking in circles); Reverse Tracking (Alex walking through the shopping mall to the music shop. Alex and his droogs walking by the pool. Georgie and Dim, now police, walking through the forest); Zoom Out (The opening shot is a close-up of Alex, staring, tracking out to see his droogs in the bar drinking moloko); Speeded Up (When Alex takes two girls home for a bit of the old in-out in-out, the footage is speeded up); Slow Motion (When Alex throws Georgie and Dim into the water, then slices Dim's hand, it is all in slow motion. When Dim retaliates with a moloko bottle in the face, outside the health farm, it is in slow-mo); Point Of View (As well as the voice-over, we constantly see things from Alex's point of view. For example, when he jumps out the window, we fall to the ground with him).

Audio Ideas: Voice-over (Alex talks to us throughout the movie); The Waltz/Dancing (Alex dances whilst singing 'Singin' In The Rain' and kicking the writer).

Themes: Hand-To-Hand (The rumble with the rival gang. Beating up Georgie & Dim); Nice To Animals (Alex has a pet snake called Basil. The woman at the health farm has lots of cats); The Beast In Man (Like Spartacus and the apes in *2001*, Alex is crouched, holding a stick in his hand when fighting); Staring/Eyes (Alex stares defiantly at us in the opening shot. Alex stares at the singer in the bar. Later, when undergoing the Ludovico Treatment Alex's eyes are kept open in terror); Theatre (Alex craves an audience - if not his droogs, then members of the establishment or the press. The rumble with the rival gang is in a theatre. Alex rapes the writer's wife, ensuring that the writer is watching. Alex is forced to watch the cinema. Alex is tested for aversion to sex and violence in front of a crowd. Alex thinks of himself making love in front of a crowd); Masks/Disguise (Alex and his droogs wear masks with phallic noses when they assault the couple. When Alex falls into the soup, drugged by the writer, his face has a kind of mask. The writer has exaggerated facial expressions); The 18th Century (At the end, when Alex is cured, he thinks of himself making love to a woman, being applauded by people with 18th-century clothing); Bars (The Korova Milkbar); Artificial Bodies (The female figures in the Korova Milkbar); Technology (Ludovico Treatment); The Paralysed Man/Illness (The writer is in a wheelchair after Alex's attack); The Collapse Of Society (The streets are desolate, strewn with litter and the elevators don't work. Alex and his droogs commit lots of crimes and get away with them); Family Relationships (Alex's parents do not know what he is up to, and don't pay much attention to him. When he is 'reformed' they don't take him back, but they feel guilty about it); CRM 114 (CRM - say each letter quickly and it becomes 'serum.' Alex is given Serum 114 for the Ludovico Treatment).

Subtext: Simply, we all have the right to free will, even the worst of us. In this particular case we are shown Alex's will. It is Alex's choice to show us the world through his eyes. This results in some pretty bizarre imagery. For example, the rumble with the rival gang is not a real fight but a mock-fight, similar to the bar fights you often see in John Ford Westerns - people flying all over the place, bottle smashing in the face, furniture breaking. This is borne out by his dream later that night when he conjures imagery from westerns, disaster movies, vampire flicks and so on. Even when reading *The Bible*, Alex thinks of whipping and fighting and sex. The excessive violence and aggressive sexual imagery in the movie comes directly from Alex's adolescent mind - a mind which has not yet learnt to adhere to the morals and mores of the society it lives within. So, Kubrick's 'message' seems to be "I do not agree with the things Alex thinks, but I defend his right to think them."

Background: Anthony Burgess wanted to use the Cockney expression 'As queer as a clockwork orange' in a book. Later, thinking about all the Teddy Boys, Mods and Rockers - British street gangs who were fighting on the beaches of England during the late 1950s/early 1960s - Burgess decided to write about them. He set it in the near-future, 1970, and wrote it in Nadsat, an imaginary street language derived from Russian. Burgess found the book difficult to write because at the heart of it was the attack on the writer's wife - it was based on an attack on Burgess' wife by four American deserters during World War Two, which caused her to miscarry. Published in 1962, the novella did not make an enormous impact.

This was Kubrick's first solo script and he followed the book very closely, often word for word. He changed elements - the girls Alex picks up in the music shop are his age, not 10-years-olds as in the book - but the sense of the book was retained. Kubrick had read the American version of the novel for which the editor decided not to include the final chapter, the chapter where Alex starts thinking about getting married, settling down to a normal life and becomes part of the community, as all teenage rebels are wont to do. Burgess' comment: "A vindication of free will had become an exaltation of the urge to sin."

The film was shot over the winter of 1970/1971 for $2 million. Most of it was shot on location, using the most futuristic architecture in Britain and then dirtying it up to look like a slum. For McDowell the most gruelling scene was when he was undergoing the Ludovico Treatment, eyelids clamped open, a (real) doctor administering fluid to his eyes so that they stayed lubricated. One of his corneas was scratched and McDowell was temporarily blinded. Upon his return, Kubrick commented that he would favour McDowell's good eye when composing the shots.

The world was shocked by *A Clockwork Orange*. A few mainstream films had begun to be awarded the dreaded X certificate including *Midnight Cowboy* (1969, director John Schlesinger) which won Oscars, *Straw Dogs* (1971, director Sam Peckinpah) and *The Devils* (1971, director Ken Russell). The X generally indicated the film was pornographic and had no artistic merit. But these films tended to disprove that theory, although it must be said that in the UK critics loved *A Clockwork Orange* and hated *Straw Dogs*.

After its initial run, Kubrick pulled *A Clockwork Orange* from the UK market in 1974 and it was never, legally, shown there until after Kubrick's death. The reason? There were many copycat incidents of ultra-violence, where people said the film made them do awful things. Complete rubbish of course, since each sane person has free will, but the press lapped it all up. Kubrick decided to stop the film (and by extension him) being blamed for something it(he) did not do and pulled it.

Kubrick once explained that people like violence, but they don't like to acknowledge that they like it. The Hollywood film-maker's job is to set things up in a movie so that when the violence occurs it has been sugar-coated enough for the viewer to readily devour it. In *A Clockwork Orange*, Kubrick does not hide the fact that Alex is evil and enjoys being evil.

And Another Thing: Why did Kubrick have such a good relationship with Warner Brothers? There was a power struggle within Warner Brothers and the marketing strategy of *A Clockwork Orange* was the battleground. *A Clockwork Orange* was released to poor grosses. Kubrick showed them computer printouts comparing these grosses with those of *2001*, which was distributed by MGM. Kubrick said they would either market it his way, or he would take the film away from them. Warner Brothers caved. By following Kubrick's plan they made a lot of money - on a budget of $2 million, by 1979 *A Clockwork Orange* grossed $40 million. From that moment on, master strategist Kubrick had complete control over his own films.

Legacies: As well as Alex recreating the slow-mo ape triumphant from *2001: A Space Odyssey*, there is also an album cover from *2001* in the music shop. That music shop has a top ten chart which includes groups like The Sparks and Heaven 17 - these real-life groups took their names from the film.

The Verdict: I have mixed views on this film. The wit and black humour of the storytelling encourage you to watch the repulsive Alex and his droogs doing their stuff. Alex is the creative one, who likes Beethoven, and I'm reminded of Maurice's words to Johnny in *The Killing*: "I often thought that the gangster and the artist are the same in the eyes of the masses. They are admired and hero-worshipped, but there is always present an underlying wish to see them destroyed at the peak of their glory." Kubrick said that he saw Alex as a kind of Richard III, who could win the audience over with his wit and honesty. He didn't win me over, I'm afraid. 3/5

Barry Lyndon (1975)

Cast: Ryan O'Neal (Barry Lyndon, born Redmond Barry), Marisa Berenson (Lady Lyndon), Patrick Magee (The Chevalier), Hardy Krüger (Captain Potzdorf), Steven Berkoff (Lord Ludd), Gay Hamilton (Nora), Marie Kean (Barry's Mother), Frank Middlemass (Sir Charles Lyndon), André Morell (Lord Wendover), Arthur O'Sullivan (Highwayman), Godfrey Quigley (Captain Grogan), Leonard Rossiter (Captain Quin), Philip Stone (Graham), Leon Vitali (Lord Bullingdon), David Morley (Brian Lyndon), Dominic Savage (Lord Bullingdon, younger), Michael Hordern (Narrator)

Crew: Director & Writer & Producer Stanley Kubrick, Novel William Makepeace Thackeray, Executive Producer Jan Harlan, Associate Producer Bernard Williams, Music The Chieftains & Leonard Rosenman, Cinematographer John Alcott, Editor Tony Lawson, Production Design Ken Adam, Historical Advisor John Mollo, 184 minutes

Story: Part One: How Redmond Barry became Barry Lyndon. Ireland, in the middle of the 18th century. Redmond Barry's father is killed in a duel, so his mother vows to protect him. Redmond falls in love with his cousin Nora Brady, a flirt. Playing cards, Redmond wins, so Nora says he can have a ribbon secreted on her body and he can search anywhere he wishes for it. The sensitive Redmond finds it between her breasts - they kiss.

When Nora starts dancing and flirting with John Quin, redcoat soldier, Redmond becomes jealous and angry. When Nora and Quin announce their wedding, it is too much for Redmond so he forces a duel between himself and Quin. After shooting Quin, Redmond hotfoots it to Dublin to stay one step ahead of the law, but he is waylaid by a polite highwayman. Penniless, Redmond joins the redcoat army and immediately starts an argument with a large bully named Mr O'Toole. They fight bare-knuckle and Redmond wins.

Finding himself in Dunleary camp, Redmond meets Captain Grogan who was his second in the duel with Quin. Grogan reveals that Redmond did not shoot Quin, that it was a dummy bullet, that Quin fainted due to fright, that Nora and Quin have since married and that the Brady family needed the money from the marriage to pay off debts.

In Germany for the seven years war, the redcoats are slaughtered by the French and Grogan is killed. Redmond is disgusted and deserts in the uniform of a courier. After a romantic interlude with a German woman, Redmond is joined on the road to Bremmen by Captain Potzdorf, who sees that Redmond is an impostor and forces him to join the regiment. When Redmond saves Potzdorf's life during battle he is rewarded with honours and, after the war, Potzdorf gets him a job as a police spy.

Redmond's job is to become the manservant of a professional gambler by the name of The Chevalier. Pleased to see a fellow Irishman, Redmond reveals his duplicity and begins spying for The Chevalier, who earns his living cheating at cards. After a particularly nasty run-in with a Prince, Redmond and The Chevalier escape the country and become a team travelling Europe swindling money out of the upper classes. The money is paid as promissory notes and, when due, Redmond duels with the Lords to force payment. But the money is only enough to pay for their upkeep - Redmond looks for a woman to marry, someone with a lot of money.

Sir Charles Lyndon, an old man in a wheelchair, has a beautiful young wife and Redmond takes a liking to her future money. He seduces her and, six hours after they meet, she falls in love. Soon after, Sir Charles Lyndon dies.

Part Two: How Barry Lyndon lost everything through misfortunes and disasters. One year later, on June 15 1773, the Reverend Samuel Runt marries the young couple. Afterwards, in the coach, Lady Lyndon complains to Barry about his pipe smoke. He turns to her and blows smoke into her face. Her 10-year-old son, Lord Bullingdon, knows that Barry is a mere opportunist. They soon have their own son, Brian. Meanwhile, Barry makes love to other women, including the maid, which is seen by Lady Lyndon. She is truly in love with Barry and her heart breaks. As she bathes, Barry enters, kisses her tenderly and says he is sorry. Barry is enchanted by all the things his new-found wealth can buy. When Lord Bullingdon is impudent, Barry gives him several strokes of a cane.

Eight years later, Barry tells his son Brian adventurous stories of derring-do - he is a good father. More than money, Barry wants a title, since he has no title of his own, and the money is owned and controlled by Lady Lyndon. He endeavours to obtain a title through Lord Wendover and others - each of these 'gentlemen' requires a gift, or bribe, or land to be bought from them at 10 times the real cost. The financial drain on the estate becomes ruinous.

When Lord Bullingdon becomes impatient with his younger brother, he beats him. Barry dislikes this so he beats Bullingdon in turn. During a formal musical recital by Lady Lyndon in front of everybody of importance, Lord Bullingdon enters with Brian. Brian is wearing Lord Bullingdon's shoes, which make a loud noise, drown out the music and stop the recital. Brian smiles, thinking it is just a game. Barry erupts, attacks Bullingdon and has to be held back.

This outburst in front of restrained society turns Barry into an outcast. His 'friends' make their excuses and turn down dinner and visiting invitations, believing Barry to be some sort of ogre. His debts begin to mount. Contrasting to this is Barry's joy at being with Brian - Barry secretly buys him a horse for his birthday, and asks a farmer to break it in. Brian finds out about the horse, sneaks out to ride it before it is ready, falls off and dies as a result of his injuries. The parents are broken by this - Barry finds solace in drink, Lady Lyndon becomes even more devoted to the church and eventually tries to poison herself.

Barry's mother comes to look after the house and the accounts. Church, the accountant, brings Lady Lyndon to Lord Bullingdon. Now that she is safe, Bullingdon finds Barry in a drinking bar and challenges him to a duel. They duel in a church. Bullingdon's pistol goes off accidentally, so Barry fires into the ground. Instead of receiving satisfaction, Bullingdon continues and shoots Barry in the leg, which a doctor says must come off. Barry's mother rushes to his side, they play cards, then Church arrives with an ultimatum: Bullingdon is offering them 500 guineas a year to get out of the country, otherwise his creditors will put him in jail when they catch up with them. After several years in Ireland, Barry spends the rest of his life gambling in Europe.

As Lady Lyndon signs Barry's cheque for 500 guineas, she pauses to reflect on her lost love. Lord Bullingdon sees that she really loved Barry. The end note makes the point that they are all equal now.

Visual Ideas: Symmetry (Virtually every scene has a symmetry and order to it); Hand-Held (The bare-knuckle fight. The battle with the French. Barry's attack on Bullingdon); Single Light Source (Most scenes are lit using natural light i.e. the sun or candles); Reverse Tracking (Potzdorf walking through the ruins. Lord Bullingdon walking through the drinking club looking for Barry); Zoom (There are too many to list here, but the duel between Redmond and Quin begins with a close-up of two guns and zooms out to reveal the men in the landscape).

Audio Ideas: Voice-over (The cynical, worldly voice of Michael Hordern narrates throughout); The Waltz/Dancing (Irish folk tunes are used when Nora and Quin are dancing. There are music recitals).

Themes: Hand-To-Hand (Redmond fights bare-knuckle with Mr O'Toole over a drink, just as his duel with Quin was over a drink of wine); Nice To Animals (Brian loves horses); Staring/Eyes (Redmond stares at Mrs Lyndon across the gaming table); Theatre (The magic act for Brian's birthday); Games (Redmond & Nora play cards for love, whereas for the rest of his life Redmond plays cards for money. Barry and his son Brian fish, duel and play croquet. At the end, Barry and his mother play cards in the inn); Masks/Disguise (Everybody wears face powder. The Chevalier wears an eyepatch); The 18th Century (This is all set in the 18th century!); Technology (The duelling pistols, which do not work properly - one being loaded without a bullet, and another going off before aiming); The Fatal Flaw (Redmond knows how to acquire money, but not how to acquire acceptance within the upper class); The Paralysed Man/Illness (The Chevalier has an eyepatch. Sir Charles Lyndon is in a wheelchair. Brian Lyndon dies after a fall, and Barry loses a leg after his duel with Lord Bullingdon); The Collapse Of Society (It doesn't - however, in the last scene, the date of the cheque to Barry is 4 December 1789, four months after the class system in France ended); Family Relationships (Redmond loves his mother and his son, Brian. Lady Lyndon loves Barry and her son, Lord Bullingdon. Lord Bullingdon loves his mother but hates his stepfather. This is not a functional family).

Subtext: This is the age of the landscaped garden, when man attempts to control nature, to make it fit into calm patterns. In a similar way, man is trying to control his own nature by building an elaborate etiquette of behaviour. However, all he is doing is masking his true nature. The polite highwayman who steals everything but Redmond's boots is the same as the polite Lords who allow him to bribe them for no return.

The other story is one of love. Redmond Barry fell in love with Nora and found himself abused by it. He travels the world and learns that the world is a bad place. From that moment on, he does not allow himself the luxury of loving. When he does - he lavishes his attention on his son - Brian dies. Barry is broken again.

And then there is the story of class. Barry is from the middle class and has no other ambition than to make money, which he is suited to do. He is at home both fighting as the lower class do (bare-knuckle) and as the upper class do (duel with pistols or swords). Even when he is married to Lady Lyndon, he is still in a lower class because he has no money of his own (she holds the purse strings) and has no title. In trying to acquire his new class, he spends a lot of money but, in the end he shows his true class when he fights bare-knuckle with Lord Bullingdon. Previously, Barry had been tolerated rather than accepted - now he is shunned. You can never acquire a new class - you always remain the class you were born into.

Background: Security was tight on *Barry Lyndon*. The press were simply told that Kubrick was making a film with Ryan O'Neal and Marisa Berenson. No title was given and no subject matter. The reason for this was simply that William Makepeace Thackeray's novel was in the public domain and any Tom, Dick or Alan Smithee could shamelessly produce a quick rip-off before Kubrick released his version.

Kubrick decided that it would be nice to capture the world of the 18th century - the time before the electric light - in its natural light. After so many years of artificiality, he wanted to film in natural light with candles only, so Kubrick helped invent lenses and cameras which amazed the industry. There was so little light going through the camera that the operators couldn't see the image for focusing. The solution? Kubrick attached a video camera to the film camera.

All the locations are real - no sets were built. Ireland was used for both Irish and German scenes. Kubrick sent a second unit to Pottsdam and East Berlin for background material, and told them what to film by using grid references on photos from location shoots. In England, Castle Howard doubled as Barry Lyndon's house. Many of the houses were open to the public so Kubrick sometimes had to film between guided tours. The costumes are authentic from the period, spruced up and slightly enlarged since people were smaller in the past. The wigs were made from the hair of young Italian girls entering religious life.

Filming in Ireland stopped because Kubrick and O'Neal received threats from the IRA - they were featuring English soldiers in Ireland.

The most striking feature of the film is the use of the zoom lens, which concentrates on a small human element, and then smoothly zooms out to reveal a panorama of nature. This fluid motion is courtesy of a joystick control, which gives the film a gentle pace. Many of the images have a familiar look to them. This is because Kubrick recreated images from the great painters of the era: Watteau, Gainsborough, Hogarth, Reynolds, Chardin and Stubbs among them.

170 cast and crew spent 8 and a half months in vans travelling from one location to another. It cost $11 million to make and premièred on 18 December 1975. Expensive film. Box-office flop.

The Verdict: This film is brilliant and probably Kubrick's most underrated film. There are beautiful images, but there is also emotional depth. 5/5

The Shining (1980)

Cast: Jack Nicholson (Jack Torrance), Shelley Duvall (Wendy Torrance), Danny Lloyd (Danny Torrance), Scatman Crothers (Dick Hallorann), Barry Nelson (Stuart Ullman), Philip Stone (Delbert Grady), Joe Turkel (Lloyd)

Crew: Director & Producer Stanley Kubrick, Writers Stanley Kubrick & Diane Johnson, Novel Stephen King, Executive Producer Jan Harlan, Music Wendy Carlos & Rachel Elkind, Additional Music Béla Bartók & Hector Berlioz & György Ligeti & Krzysztof Penderecki, Cinematographer John Alcott, Editor Ray Lovejoy, Production Design Roy Walker, Steadicam Operators Garrett Brown & Ted Churchill, 119 and 146 minutes

Story: The Interview: Writer Jack Torrance has an interview for the position of winter caretaker with the manager of the Overlook Hotel. He is told about the tragedy in 1970 when the caretaker, Delbert Grady, killed his wife and two girls before taking his own life. "You can be rest assured it won't happen to me," Jack says.

Back at home, his son Danny sees visions of blood, twins and himself screaming. A doctor examines him when he comes out of his trance, and his mother Wendy explains to the doctor that Jack hurt Danny once, dislocated his arm when drunk, but Jack is on the wagon now.

Closing Day: Travelling to the hotel, the family talk about the Donner Party, a group of pioneers who got lost in the mountains and had to resort to cannibalism to survive. Arriving they are shown around the hotel and the maze behind - when everybody is gone it'll be "just like a ghost ship." Danny sees the twin girls he previously saw in his vision. Danny is left with Dick Hallorann, the cook. Dick and Danny both have ESP, and Dick explains it to Danny calling it 'shining.' Danny asks what is wrong with room 237. Dick does not answer.

A Month Later: We follow Danny on his bike, roving the corridors. Jack looks in the mirror. Jack says, "I feel as though I've been here before." Jack cannot write - he walks over to a scale model of the maze, looks down and sees Danny and Wendy in the centre of the maze.

Tuesday: Snow is on the way and soon they will be cut off. On his bike, Danny arrives at room 237. He has a vision of the twins. Jack is typing away at his novel when Wendy disturbs him - he is upset that she is breaking his concentration and shouts at her.

Thursday: The snow is here. Jack is staring into space.

Saturday: The phone lines are down for the winter so radio is their only form of communication. Danny rides into a corridor and sees the twins. "Come and play with us, Danny, for ever and ever and ever," they say, then Danny sees their slaughtered bodies on the floor. When Danny later sneaks into his father's bedroom, Jack cuddles him and says, "I wish we could stay here forever and ever." Jack promises Danny that he would never hurt him or his mother.

Wednesday: Danny is playing when he sees the door to room 237 open and goes in. Wendy is in the basement when she hears Jack screaming in his sleep. He wakes saying he had a terrible nightmare in which he was killing her and Danny. Danny enters with a bruised neck - Wendy accuses Jack. "Not me," Jack says. He wanders into The Gold Room, a big ballroom, and sits at the empty bar, and says: "I'd give my goddamn soul for a glass of beer." Lloyd, the barman serves Jack a drink. Wendy enters carrying a baseball bat (Lloyd is not there) and says that a woman strangled Danny. "Are you out of your fucking mind?" Jack asks, pointing out that there is nobody else in the hotel, but goes to investigate. Jack enters room 237, sees a beautiful naked woman, kisses her and, in the mirror, sees she is a decomposing old woman. At the same time, Danny 'talks' to Dick and shows him room 237, the bathroom, blood, keeps saying "Redrum" - Dick decides to make his way from Florida back to the Overlook. Jack goes back to the ballroom, which is full of people, and Grady spills avocado on Jack's jacket. In the bathroom, Grady says that Jack has always been the caretaker, and that Danny's power is bringing the "nigger" back to the hotel. Grady explains that he had to "correct" his wife and daughters, and perhaps Jack should "correct" his wife and son.

8 a.m.: Dick is on the plane to the Overlook. Jack is typing furiously. Dick gets a snow-cat. Wendy sees Jack's novel - it is the sentence 'All work and no play makes Jack a dull boy' repeated endlessly in different patterns. Jack catches her, menacing, saying that he has an obligation to his employers, that he has his future, his responsibilities to think about, and Wendy is interfering with that. Wendy knocks Jack on the head and he falls down the stairs. She drags him to the food locker and locks him in. She finds out Jack has ruined the radio and disabled the snow-cat.

4 p.m.: Outside the food locker, Grady wonders whether Jack has "the belly" for the work. Grady unlocks the door and lets Jack out, who is limping from his fall. Dick is on his way in the snow-cat. Wendy is asleep, exhausted. In a trance, Danny writes 'REDRUM' on the door with lipstick. Wendy wakes, sees it spells 'MURDER' in the mirror, screams, an axe starts splitting the door. Jack is the big bad wolf. Danny slides out the bathroom window. Wendy is trapped in the bathroom. Jack splits the door and puts his head through shouting "Heeeeere's Johnny!" Wendy slices his hand with a knife. Jack hears Dick's snow-cat arrive. Dick walks in, gets an axe in his chest and dies. Danny runs into the maze. Wendy runs upstairs and sees perverse ghosts. Jack chases Danny through the maze. Wendy sees a man covered in blood, then ghosts in the lounge, then a river of blood pours from the escalators. Wendy stares in horror. Danny walks in his own footsteps, then follows his tracks back out. Jack gets lost. Danny and Wendy escape in the snow-cat.

The next day: Jack is frozen in the maze, staring. We travel to a photo on the wall of the hotel, a 4 July Ball in 1921, and in the centre of the picture is Jack, smiling.

Visual Ideas: Mirrors (The opening shot of the water is like a mirror. Danny is looking in the mirror when he has a vision. Jack is often seen in the mirror of the Torrance room. Jack sees the ugly ghost in the mirror. REDRUM is MURDER in the mirror); Corridors (It's a hotel so there are miles of corridors. The maze); Symmetry (Virtually every scene has horizontal or vertical symmetry); Film Noir/Expressionism (The whole film is very light but the scene where Jack leaves room 237 is backlit like film noir); Hand-Held (Technically, most of the movie is hand-held, but there are no jerky hand-helds in this); Reverse Tracking (At danger points there is a lot of reverse tracking - the whole movie is done like this); Signs (When Danny sees the twins dead on the floor, they are under an exit sign); Patterns (The Native American designs on the rugs and carpets throughout the hotel look like mazes, like the hotel is a maze); Power (When Grady talks to Jack in the bathroom, at first we see Jack and do not see Grady's face, which gives Jack a lot of power. When we go to Grady's face, he begins to dominate, and takes the power from the scene. Very clever film-making and acting - Philip Stone as Grady is very menacing).

Audio Ideas: Natural Sound (When Danny is riding his bike and going over wood and rugs, the rhythmic noise gives a strangely unsettling effect); Music (Like *2001*, strange whining, strangling sounds are used to create an unsettled atmosphere, only more of it is used here).

Themes: Hand-To-Hand (Wendy and Jack argue - I don't think they touch, kiss or show any affection towards each other in the whole movie); Staring/Eyes (Jack, Danny, Wendy and Dick all take turns staring, but Jack wins); Theatre (TV is on all the time); Games (Danny plays with his cars, darts, baseball bat, balloons and drives his bike); Masks/Disguise (The beautiful/ugly ghost. Jack smiling maniacally when his head is through the bathroom door); Bars (Lloyd at the bar in the Gold Room); Artificial Bodies (The ghosts); Technology (The phone lines are down. Jack disables the radio and snow-cat); The Fatal Flaw (Jack cannot control his temper); The Paralysed Man/Illness (Jack hurts his leg so limps after Danny and Wendy, and he is 'paralysed' at the end); Family Relationships (This is one helluva dysfunctional family - avoid at all costs).

Subtext: The most annoying thing about this movie is that it is very satisfying to watch, but almost completely incomprehensible when analysed - it's a waking dream. I've been trying to work out what is the key scene or defining moment but it proves elusive. My best guess is when Dick Hallorann explains about The Shining/ESP to Danny. Perhaps the following makes sense...

We have two separate concepts. First ESP/shining, which is Danny's alarm system. Second is a haunted house where, as Dick says, "When something happens it can leave traces behind."

As in *2001*, the outside force (the aliens/haunted house) acts on the humans so that they reveal their true nature. In the case of Jack - he is angry and frustrated by his inability to work, to be creative, and the house accentuates this anger, it uses Jack's repressed feelings against him and gradually possesses him. Jack wants to drink and do violence. The house gives him the opportunity and excuse to carry out these desires and hence turn against his family. Danny has ESP, and the house acts on him through that power - it shows him the twins and asks him to join them. (Danny is also a twin, having an imaginary friend called Tony.) Wendy is docile and ineffective, but she is the one who uses the house most - she makes dinner, looks after the boiler, operates the radio. She is the last to know what is going on and the last to see the horrors of the house.

Dick says that he talked to his mother without speaking, so perhaps ESP is passed on from generation to generation. In the case of the Torrance family, it is from father to son, only both refuse to recognise the power. The father represses all acts of creativity and vision, hence is unable to write. The son creates an imaginary friend, Tony, to account for his visions.

There is a hint that the hotel collects people like Jack, people who have 'troubled minds' like family killer Grady. Grady says that Jack was the killer, which brings up another idea, that Jack is reincarnated, reborn, damned to repeatedly kill his own family. Perhaps the traces are the re-enactments with whomsoever inhabits the house.

Whatever the 'proper' explanation, this is probably Kubrick's bleakest examination of the dysfunctional family. Things must be bad if a father is willing to kill both his wife and son. In this case, the killer instinct has gone amok.

Background: The Timberline Lodge on Mount Hood in Oregon was used for exteriors of the Overlook Hotel, and all the interiors were built in Britain. For each hotel room the decor was picked by Kubrick - he had thousands of photos to choose from because location scouts had visited hundreds of hotel to get an authentic look. The management of the Timberline Lodge requested that Kubrick did not use room 217 (as specified in the book) - they were afraid nobody would want to stay in that room ever again. Kubrick changed the room number to the non-existent 237.

The Shining looked completely different to other movies thanks to Garrett Brown, inventor and operator of the Steadicam. He had used the new camera to get smooth travelling shots in *Rocky* (1976, director John G Avildsen) and *Marathon Man* (1976, director John Schlesinger). Now he had a better version, one that could be put lower to the ground. Kubrick seized on it immediately - it would be ideal for Danny's lowdown view of the world. Kubrick could put the camera anywhere on the set he wanted even 1 inch from a wall. Brown got the job of shooting most of the film, even still shots, because he could put the camera in positions ordinary cameras could not go.

As usual, Kubrick asked for many takes of each scene - Scatman Crothers once did 148 takes. Different actors had different ideas about why. Some thought that he got better performances out of extremity and exhaustion. For example, Steven Berkoff (who appeared in *A Clockwork Orange*) believed the repetition meant that the actor forgot he was saying lines, forgot to act and became the part - Kubrick was going for realism through slight nuances of performances. Brown said he loved doing the repeated number of takes because he developed a muscle memory using the camera, and found that he could operate it more effectively.

Nicholson, a former writer himself, remembered a time when he was arguing with his then-wife and incorporated emotional outbursts into the script. For example, "Just because you don't hear the typewriter doesn't mean I'm not writing." The now-famous line said when he puts his head through the bathroom door, "Here's Johnny!" was ad libbed by Nicholson.

Filming took place between May 1978 and April 1979, with the première in May 1980. At the last minute, Kubrick decided to end on Jack in the 1921 photo of the Overlook Hotel, which meant cutting the last scene between Wendy and the hotel manager. The problem was, prints had already been released, so Kubrick got film editors to get on their bikes and personally cut the film from the prints. Previously, Kubrick's films had opened small and built by word of mouth, but the large $10-15 million budget on *The Shining* meant that Warner Brothers had to do a media blitz to recover their money. The negative reviews were offset by great box office - the opening weekend grossed $1 million, which was better than Warner Brothers' previous blockbusters *The Exorcist* (1973) and *Superman* (1978).

The Verdict: I enjoy this movie each time I see it because of Jack Nicholson's performance, the prowling camerawork and the overwhelming sense of menace. I don't think it is meant to make complete sense because it is a waking nightmare. 4/5

Full Metal Jacket (1987)

Cast: Matthew Modine (Private Joker/ Private J T Davis), Adam Baldwin (Animal Mother), Vincent D'Onofrio (Private Gomer Pyle/ Private Leonard Lawrence), R Lee Ermey (Gunnery Sergeant Hartman), Dorian Harewood (Eightball), Arliss Howard (Cowboy Kevyn), Major Howard (Rafterman), Ed O'Ross (Lt. Walter J Tinoshky/Lt. Touchdown), John Terry (Lt. Lockhart), Kieron Jecchinis (Crazy Earl), Bruce Boa (Pogue), Colonel Kirk Taylor (Payback), Jon Stafford (Doc Jay), Peter Edmund (Private Snowball/ Private Brown), Vivian Kubrick (uncredited News Camera Operator at Mass Grave)

Crew: Director & Producer Stanley Kubrick, Writers Gustav Hasford & Michael Herr & Stanley Kubrick, Novel *The Short-Timers* Gustav Hasford, Executive Producer Jan Harlan, Associate Producer Michael Herr, Co-Producer Philip Hobbs, Music Vivian Kubrick (as Abigail Mead), Cinematographer Douglas Milsome, Editor Martin Hunter, Production Design Anton Furst, Technical Advisor R Lee Ermey, 116 minutes

Story: After their haircuts, platoon 3092 undergo training at Parris Island, South Carolina. They are shouted at and insulted and hit and embarrassed and shamed and bullied by Gunnery Sergeant Hartman. He names them Private Joker and Cowboy and Gomer Pyle etc. Private Pyle has a smirk on his face so Hartman chokes him until the smirk goes. They run, sounding off, repeating Hartman's words. On parade, Pyle does not know his left from right so Hartman hits him. Pyle has to march behind the platoon with his trousers down to his ankles, his rifle upside down and his thumb in his mouth. They sleep with their rifles. They give their rifles female names. They pray to their rifles. On the obstacle course, Pyle quits - he is too fat - and Hartman shouts at him. Joker does not believe in the Virgin Mary, so Hartman shouts at him to change his mind, which Joker does not, so Hartman makes him Squad Leader and tells Joker to look after Pyle. Pyle may be dumb but, Hartman says, "he's got guts."

Joker teaches Pyle about his rifle, lacing his shoes, making his bed, getting over obstacles, parading and Pyle does well. Then Hartman finds a jelly doughnut in Pyle's footlocker - from now on if Pyle fucks up the rest of the platoon pays for it. That night, the platoon put soap in towels, hold Pyle down and beat him. Joker beats him as well.

Hartman tells them that Charles Whitman, who killed 12 people at up to 400 yards, and Lee Harvey Oswald, who shot the President twice, learnt to shoot in the Marines. Pyle's mind has gone.

The Marines sing happy birthday to Jesus. "We keep Heaven packed with fresh souls - our present to Jesus."

Pyle starts talking to his rifle. He is a marksman, he is becoming a killer. Joker: "The Marines do not want robots, they want killers, men without fear."

They graduate, and get their orders. On the last night, Joker has fire-watch, and finds Pyle in the head (toilets) with a gun and live rounds. ("7.62 millimetre with full metal jacket.") Pyle: "I am in a world of shit." Hartman enters: "What's this Mickey Mouse shit?" Pyle shoots Hartman dead, then puts the rifle barrel in his mouth and pulls the trigger.

Vietnam: Joker and his photographer friend Rafterman work for *Stars And Stripes*, the Army newspaper, where their job is to write propaganda not the truth. When Joker jokes, the other journalists don't take him seriously, because he doesn't have the 1000-yard stare that a grunt has when he's been in country too long. The Tet holiday ceasefire is violated - US Army bases are attacked all over, dividing the country in half. Joker and Rafterman report on a mass grave, and then join a squad - Joker meets his old buddy Cowboy. He meets tough guy Animal Mother, plus Eightball, Doc Jay, Payback and Lieutenant Touchdown. About the Vietnamese: "These people are the finest human beings…We're going to miss them."

On the road, they make their way to the city of Hue, and clean out one section. Standing in a circle over two dead soldiers, Animal Mother says, "Better you than me." A film crew interviews each of them. A hooker comes on a motorbike, and charges $5 each.

On patrol in bombed-out Hue city, the Lieutenant picks up a bunny rabbit, BOOM, booby-trapped, he's gone. Cowboy is the new leader. They get lost. Investigating a new area, Eightball gets shot by a sniper. He's down out in the open. The squad can do nothing as he's shot twice more. Doc Jay goes in to rescue Eightball and is shot. Animal Mother spearheads a way around to get at the sniper. Cowboy is radioing HQ when he is shot. He dies. Animal throws in smoke bombs to cover their advance across open ground. Joker finds the sniper, a young woman, but his rifle jams. She shoots at him. He's trapped behind a post. Rafterman shoots her. The squad look at her as she dies slowly, praying, asking to be shot. Joker shoots her. He's 'hardcore.' Rafterman is very pleased he shot the gook, and wants to make sure he gets the kill confirmed. Rafterman has the stare now, and so does Joker. They are killers.

Walking off into the night, the squad sing the theme tune to *The Mickey Mouse Club* TV show. Joker: "I am in a world of shit, yes, but I am alive, and I am not afraid."

Visual Ideas: Symmetry (Barracks); Hand-Held (I think Kubrick fell in love with the smooth Steadicam, which means you don't get the vicarious feeling of being there that documentary-like jerky movements have. Just look at the battle scenes in *Dr Strangelove* for a comparison); Circles (Circular doors in Vietnam. The squad stand in a circle around two dead bodies); Reverse Tracking (Hartman walking. The platoon running and on parade. Advancing on the road. Advancing on patrol).

Audio Ideas: Voice-over (Occasional); Language (There is very specific jargon used by the Army and the soldiers also have their own language - very reminiscent of *A Clockwork Orange*).

Themes: Hand-To-Hand (During training they fight hand-to-hand, but this is a long-range war fought with tools called rifles); Staring/Eyes (Hartman stares all the time. Pyle when Hartman explains about Whitman and Oswald. Then Pyle again in the head. Most of the grunts have stares. Joker stares at the end when shooting the sniper); Theatre (Hartman is playing a role. Theatre of war); Masks/Disguise (The journalists pretend to tell the truth); Technology (Rifles); The Fatal Flaw (Joker tries to make political and moral sense out of a situation that has no politics or morals. He must kill or be killed. He has been trained to kill, and now he must survive by using his training and not thinking about it. So thinking is his flaw); The Paralysed Man/Illness (Pyle is mentally ill); The Collapse Of Society (Parris Island has brutal rules but it is safe. The world of Army journalism is hypocritical and unfair but safe. The field of combat is without rules or friends and your only concern is your own survival); Family Relationships (The only family is in Parris Island, and they are lost one by one throughout the war); Mickey Mouse (When Hartman enters the head to confront Joker and Pyle, he cries "What is this Mickey Mouse shit?" and at the end, the squad sing the theme from *The Mickey Mouse Club* as they march through the burning city).

Subtext: This is about the decision to kill, and the loss of humanity. The purpose of the first third is to show how people are trained to be killers. This dehumanising process results in dumb Private Pyle going mad and shooting himself because he cannot bear to live. The second third shows Private Joker as a journalist witnessing the bad things happening in Vietnam. This is structurally weak but, time and again, we are shown how the military command are failing to deal with the situation. Joker talks the talk but cannot walk the walk - he has not seen combat. The final third shows how people become killers. Joker finds out, first-hand, what it is like to watch people being killed. When it comes to combat, Joker fails - all that training was for nothing - because he still has intelligence and humanity. As an act of humanity, he kills the female sniper. His first kill comes out of compassion for his fellow human beings, not hatred. Joker's dual nature, as killer and compassionate human, is evoked through his attire ('Born To Kill' on helmet, Peace badge on chest) and his words (in an interview Joker says he "wanted to see exotic Vietnam, the jewel of Southeast Asia. I wanted to meet interesting, stimulating people of an ancient culture, and kill them").

Background: In 1980, Kubrick contacted Michael Herr, author of a book about the Indochina war *Dispatches*, and the guy who wrote Martin Sheen's narration for *Apocalypse Now* (1979, director Francis Ford Coppola, script by John Milius based on Joseph Conrad's *Heart Of Darkness*). They were constantly on the phone. Herr described this period as a 3-year phone call with interruptions. Kubrick was looking for a war subject and Herr suggested Gustav Hasford's novel *The Short-Timers*, which was immediately snapped up. Hasford wrote for the script, as did Herr and Kubrick in collaboration.

As with his three previous films, Kubrick did video auditions, organised by his assistant Leon Vitali - the adult Lord Bullingdon in *Barry Lyndon*. The most amazing tape was made by Lee Ermey. A former Marines drill instructor in Vietnam for 30 months, in 1969 a rocket exploded bedding shrapnel into his back and arm. With his sick pay, he bought a brothel in Okinawa, which he turned into a drinking club. Whilst in Manila under the GI Bill in 1976, he got a part in *Apocalypse Now*, which led to other film roles. Ermey wanted the part of the drill instructor but Kubrick said he wasn't vicious enough, so Ermey got the auditioning actors together and began humiliating them, swearing at them and so on for 15 minutes. Kubrick hired him, had the tape transcribed, and used half of the dialogue in the finished film. When the shoot started, Ermey and the actors met for the first time on camera when he is shouting at them - Kubrick did this to get authentic reactions.

All the locations for Parris Island and Vietnam were found within 30 miles of Kubrick's house. The area of Beckton, which was bombed during World War Two, had been designed by the same French architects who designed the buildings in Hue. The area was owned by British Gas, and it was due for demolition, so Kubrick did the job for them. 200 palm trees were imported from Spain and 5,000 Vietnamese immigrants were found in London to appear in the background.

Filming began in summer of 1985, and ended in September of 1986. In the middle of shooting, Lee Ermey had a near-fatal jeep accident at 1 a.m., breaking all of his ribs on one side. He refused to pass out and kept flashing his car lights until a motorist stopped. Kubrick shut down the production for 5 months. In some scenes, Ermey does not move one of his arms.

When filming was complete, Kubrick added music by Abigail Mead - a pseudonym for Vivian Kubrick. She had taken the name from Abbott's Mead, where they lived, and Abigail means 'a father rejoices.' She took some flak for the music - many accused Kubrick of nepotism (Jan Harlan is Kubrick's brother-in-law, Philip Hobbs is his son-in-law) - but the discordant music is very effective and added much-needed atmosphere. She even helped turn Lee Ermey's Marine rap into a best-selling pop record, getting to number 2 in the UK singles chart.

Many filmed scenes were excised from the final cut - the mad Captain January and the decapitation of the sniper for example - which was released in June 1987. It cost $17 million, took $5.5 million in the first 10 days and grossed $30 million in the first 50 days. Kubrick had another hit on his hands.

And Another Thing: If you can get hold of a copy of Gustav Hasford's novel *The Short-Timers*, you will find yourself in for a different ride. Although many elements are the same, Hasford's book is more visceral than Kubrick's movie. Firstly, Joker's personality is stronger, more sarcastic, blacker. In the middle third of the film, he rebels against all the bullshit he has to put up with as a journalist, kills the woman sniper and is transferred to gruntdom. Finally, when the squad come under fire from a laughing sniper and Cowboy is hit, Joker becomes the squad leader and decides to shoot his friend dead. By doing this, he stops the squad going all gung ho like John Wayne and getting themselves killed performing meaningless heroic acts. He leads the squad out of trouble, waiting for the next incident for them to survive. This is far bleaker than the film.

The Verdict: After an incredible verbal and visual assault in the first 40 minutes, thanks to a superb performance by Lee Ermey, we lose interest following the bland Joker character. The horror is generally not very horrible, although the gunner indiscriminately shooting civilians from his helicopter IS scary. Interest is regained with the sniper set piece. Throughout the movie, Joker retains his humanity despite the brain-and-body-washing of the army, which gives him ethical dilemmas at the end. He consoles himself that he is still living, although it is in Hell. 3/5

Eyes Wide Shut (1999)

Cast: Tom Cruise (Dr Bill Harford), Nicole Kidman (Alice Harford), Madison Eginton (Helena Harford), Marie Richardson (Marion Nathanson), Sydney Pollack (Victor Ziegler), Rade Serbedzija (Milich), Leslie Lowe (Ilona), Vinessa Shaw (Domino), Todd Field (Nick Nightingale), Alan Cumming (Hotel Desk Clerk), Sky Dumont (Sandor Szavost), Louise J Taylor (Gayle), Stewart Thorndike (Nuala), Julienne Davis (Amanda 'Mandy' Curran), Thomas Gibson (Carl), Leelee Sobieski (Milich's Daughter), Brian W Cook (Tall Butler), Leon Vitali (Red Cloak), Fay Masterson (Sally)

Crew: Director & Executive Producer Stanley Kubrick, Writers Stanley Kubrick & Frederic Raphael, Novel *Traumnovelle* Arthur Schnitzler, Producer Brian W Cook, Co-producer Jan Harlan, Original Music Jocelyn Pook, Additional Music György Ligeti & Franz Liszt & Dmitri Shostakovich, Cinematographer Larry Smith, Film Editor Nigel Galt, Production Design Leslie Tomkins & Roy Walker, Original Paintings Christiane Kubrick & Katharina Kubrick (as Katharina Hobbs), 159 minutes

Story: Alice undresses and Bill walks around the apartment getting ready. Alice is on the toilet and asks Bill if she looks okay. He says "Yes," but he's not looking. She calls him on it. On the surface, everything looks fine and dandy - they look like a beautiful couple but there is trouble brewing.

At the party, after meeting their hosts, Victor Ziegler and his wife, Alice and Bill flirt with other people. They see each other and continue flirting. Alice dances with a charming/slimy Hungarian who says, "One of the charms of marriage is that it makes deception a necessity for both parties." Bill has a beautiful model on each arm, but he is called away by

Ziegler before anything happens. In Ziegler's bathroom a naked woman, Mandy, has ODed on a combination of heroin and coke. Dr Bill revives her and makes sure she is okay. She is grateful. Dr Bill assures Ziegler that it will remain a confidential matter. Back home, Alice looks at her naked body in the mirror, while Bill tries to make love to her.

The next day is routine. Dr Bill sees and examines women (some naked), Alice is mother to their child Helena. That night, they smoke some pot and begin arguing. Alice asks if Bill fucked the two women at the dance. Bill, not being able to tell her about Ziegler, says that they were only models. On the subject of men and women, Bill says that men are driven by sex. Alice: "So you're saying men only talk to me because they want to have sex with me?" So does this apply to Bill, too? Does he want to have sex with other women but refuses their advances out of consideration for Alice? Alice explains that women like to have sex as well. She asks whether Bill's patients ever fantasise about him when he is touching them? He says that they are too worried about what he may find when examining them (this rings false) and that a nurse is always present.

Bill is sure that Alice would never betray him. She tells Bill about a holiday, seeing a Naval Officer, fantasising about him and that, if he had asked, she would have left Bill, her daughter and her life for him because her desire for him was so great. That night, on holiday, when Bill and Alice made love, Alice imagined it was the Naval Officer caressing her, inside her. The next day, she was relieved to find the Naval Officer gone.

Dr Bill receives a call - a patient has died. In the cab, Bill visualises Alice and the Officer. At the rich patient's apartment, Bill touches the head of the dead man. The dead man's daughter, Mary, describes that day, explains she is going to marry Carl and then kisses Bill saying that she loves him. (So his patients do fantasise about him.) Before anything can happen Carl arrives. (Mary and Carl look like Alice and Bill - so if Mary can love another, so can Alice.)

Bill walks through the streets. Seeing a couple kiss, he thinks of Alice and the Officer. To revenge himself, when a beautiful hooker picks him up, he goes to her room. Passive, Bill lets Domino decide what sexual acts she wants to do with him. "I'm in your hands." As they are about to kiss, the phone rings – it is Alice. Bill gives Domino $150 and they part.

Walking, Bill comes across the Sonata Café, where his friend Nick Nightingale is a pianist in a jazz band. (They went to medical school together and met at the Ziegler party where Nick was playing.) Nick says he has to go to a gig later, doesn't know where, but he plays blindfolded. One time the blindfold slipped and he saw these incredible, naked women and sexual acts... Bill wants to crash the party. The password is FIDELIO (fidelity), but Bill needs a mask and costume to enter.

It's late at night, so when Bill wakes Milich, the owner of Rainbow Fashions, he offers to pay $200 over the rental price. Among the costumes, Milich finds two Japanese cross-dressers in a sexual liaison with his 14-year-old daughter. The daughter comes on to Bill, who seems quite willing.

In the taxi, Bill thinks of Alice and her dream lover together, his visualisation becoming more explicit. He arrives at the gates of a large house, gives the password, dons cloak and mask, and walks through many doorways, into a church-like atmosphere. A man in red, with incense, chants while blessing a circle of women who are naked except for their masks. The congregation are cloaked and masked like Bill.

The women rise one by one and select a partner by kissing them. One picks Bill, recognises him and tells him he is in extreme danger. She is led away by another, so Bill continues his travels through the house, each room filled with people fucking. In one room there are male couples dancing to 'Strangers In The Night.' Female couples are in another room. The woman returns and warns Bill again, but he is led to the main room and brought before the man in red. When asked, Bill does not know the password for the house. He is unmasked and asked to undress. Then the woman asks to take Bill's place, and Bill is allowed to leave.

At home, Bill hides his costume and wakes Alice, who is having a weird dream. She says they were naked in a strange city - she sent him away for coats - then she fucked many men. (As though she could be a fantasy woman at the party.)

Determined to find out what had happened the previous night, Bill traces his footsteps. The Sonata Café is shut, so he goes to Nick's hotel - Nick left in a hurry, a bruise on his face, accompanied by two men. At Rainbow Fashions, Bill returns his costume but the mask is missing. The daughter is with the Japanese men - a financial arrangement having been made. At the gate of the large house, Bill is handed a note saying he is to give up. When he phones Mary, Carl answers. When he goes to Domino's, her roommate Sally is there and they begin foreplay, instigated by Bill, but then they stop when Sally announces Domino tested HIV positive. (Alice saved his life with her phone call because she stopped Bill having sex with Domino.)

Walking, Bill realises he is being followed and is scared. In the newspaper, he sees that Mandy - the girl he treated at Ziegler's - is in hospital. He visits but she is dead. He sees her naked body in the morgue, and bends down to kiss her, but doesn't. (He believes she saved his life at the party.)

Victor Ziegler summons Bill, says he knows about the previous night, but Bill feigns ignorance. "Please Bill, no games," Ziegler says, rolling balls around his bright red pool table, "I was there." He explains that there was no password for the house - it was a trick - that the woman who saved him was a hooker. "Suppose I said it was all staged, fake, a charade, to scare the shit out of you, to keep you quiet." He says that Mandy was the woman who saved Bill - the women whose life he saved.

Returning home, Bill finds Alice sleeping on the bed, the mask on his pillow. He cries, realising that she was only imagining, like a dream, but he was doing things for real. Bill wakes her and tells her everything. She is upset. "How could you do this to me?"

Christmas shopping with their girl, they are grateful that they survived their adventures, whether real or a dream. "One night is not the whole life," Alice says to Bill (i.e. I forgive you). "No dream is just a dream," he replies (i.e. there must be something wrong for you to have that dream). They are awake now, aware. Alice says "There's something we have to do as soon as possible… fuck."

Visual Ideas: Mirrors (Both Bill and Alice look in mirrors, and also there are mirrored relationships): Corridors; Symmetry; Film Noir/ Expressionism (When Bill is followed, the lighting, like an Edward Hopper painting, picks out his follower); Circles (The circle of naked women, and there's a game in the toyshop called The Magic Circle - referring to magicians); Reverse Tracking; Red (Sex/Depravity/Degradation/The Devil - this represents temptation and sex. The Sonata Café is painted red, the cabbie wears a red shirt, Bill is taken to the big house in a red car, the house is decorated in red, the orgy leader is in red, red flowers in the hotel, Milich's daughter leaves a blood-red room with the Japanese, Domino's front doors are red, Ziegler's pool table is red); Blue (Danger/Fear - When Bill imagines Alice and the Naval Officer it is with a blue background, as are some of his meetings with Alice); Purple (Red and Blue joined make Purple - the colour of the sheets when Bill reveals

85

all to Alice); Yellow (Betrayal/Deceit/Lies - the rooms in Ziegler's party, Marion Nathanson's apartment, Bill and Alice's bedroom).

Audio Ideas: The Waltz/Dancing (Alice dances in the opening party, and people dance at the orgy).

Themes: Staring/Eyes (Bill stares, but he is often looking down, afraid of what he might find); Theatre (The chanting and incense at the orgy is theatre); Games (Hooker called Domino. The pool table); Masks/ Disguise (There are African masks on Domino's wall. Bill goes to a costume shop. Everybody at the orgy is wearing a mask - but they recognise Bill even in his mask. Masks have eyes that are always open but they never see anything); The 18th Century (The big house); Artificial Bodies (The women at the party are treated as objects. The women in Dr Bill's surgery are objects, as are models and hookers); The Fatal Flaw (Dr Bill knows about bodies, but is so self-centred that he knows little about people's desires or thoughts); The Paralysed Man/Illness (There are two dead bodies - he touches the first, but stops himself from kissing the second because of the sexual overtones. As a doctor there should be no sexual overtones to his touching of a patient, but there are. He has begun to see his patients as people, not objects); The Collapse Of Society (If this secret society exists, then it thrives, it finds people with a lot of money willing to have unprotected sex with mysterious people. Will AIDS kill that society? Domino tested HIV positive); Family Relationships (Bill tries to get revenge for Alice's imaginary indiscretion, without thought of his daughter or consulting Alice herself about his feelings).

Subtext: Bill is so sure of Alice's fidelity, that it is shaken when she reveals herself to be something other than his fixed image of her. (The mask he puts on her?) This leads to jealousy, a feeling of betrayal and then a descent into the circles of Dante's *Inferno*, examining all the stereotypical views of women. Yet he cannot consummate any of the relationships with these 'imaginary' people, only with a 'real' woman, his wife. He must come to terms with the fact that his wife, a mother, is as sexually, emotionally and intellectually awake as he is/isn't. At the beginning, she asks if she looks okay and he answers without looking. Her confession makes him look at her. He then has his own experiences, a waking dream (an allegory for his thinking about the situation), and he confesses his thoughts to his wife. It is only when they are frank with each other that they can begin to act normally. They start with the basics - making love.

Background: After the release of *Full Metal Jacket* in 1987, Kubrick worked on several projects. For many years, Kubrick was building a story called *AI*, which stands for Artificial Intelligence. An epic science fiction story, based on Brian Aldiss' short story 'Super-Toys Last All Summer Long,' he shelved it in 1991 because the effects needed at the most basic level could not be put on the screen.

Kubrick moved on to *Aryan Papers*. Set in World War Two, it was about a Jewish boy and his aunt trying to survive in Nazi-occupied Poland by passing as Aryan. Based on Louis Begley's first novel *Wartime Lies* (1991), it was to star Joseph Mazzello (*Jurassic Park*) and rumour had it that anyone from Julia Roberts to Uma Thurman to Jodie Foster were to play the aunt. Location scouts were sent to Poland, Hungary and Slovakia where the production was to be based. A 100-day shoot was to begin in the summer of 1993 for a Christmas 1994 release, but Kubrick decided not to make it because the subject was too similar to Steven Spielberg's *Schindler's List*.

Spielberg's other movie that year, *Jurassic Park*, gave Kubrick the confidence that perhaps the special effects he wanted for *AI* could now be achieved. Set in a future where many of the world's cities are under water (the ice caps have melted due to the greenhouse effect) and robots perform many daily tasks, the focus is on a robot-like boy who wants to become a human being. Kubrick talked of it being a modern *Pinocchio*. After investigating further with special effects companies ILM and Digital Domain, in December 1995 it was announced that *AI* was in the final stages of set design and special-effects development. (After Kubrick's death *A.I. (Artificial Intelligence)* was filmed by Steven Spielberg and released in 2001.) While he was waiting, Kubrick decided to make a small film… *Eyes Wide Shut*.

Kubrick, like Hitchcock, always preferred using source novels and interpreting them in his own unique way. In this case, *Eyes Wide Shut* is based on Arthur Schnitzler's 1926 German novella *Traumnovelle*, published in English as *Rhapsody: A Dream Novel*. It's a film Kubrick had in his head for some time. In the early 1980s, when interviewed by Michel Ciment, Kubrick commented, "It's a difficult book to describe - what good book isn't? It explores the sexual ambivalence of a happy marriage and tries to equate the importance of sexual dreams and might-have-beens with reality. All of Schnitzler's work is psychologically brilliant…"

The book is set in 1920s Vienna and concerns the marriage crisis of Doctor Fridolin and his wife Albertine - the film follows the book quite closely. Kubrick to Ciment again, "The book opposes the real adventures of a husband and the fantasy adventures of his wife, and asks the question: is there a serious difference between dreaming a sexual adventure, and actually having one?"

Filming finally began 4 November 1996. As usual, Kubrick, worked on the script, rewriting scenes each day. All of the filming took place in England except for a few New York location inserts.

As well as Cruise and Kidman, Harvey Keitel and Jennifer Jason Leigh were hired at the beginning of the shoot. However, Harvey Keitel left after six months and was replaced by film director Sydney Pollack (*Jeremiah Johnson, Out Of Africa*) who acted so brilliantly in Woody Allen's *Husbands And Wives*. A new actor = reshoots. So, the Keitel scenes were refilmed in May 1997 with Sydney Pollack.

Kubrick learnt how to tell the story as he went along, he discovered each shot through the retakes and, when he understood it, moved on to the next shot. Kubrick was self-taught, he learnt photography and he learnt to make films by making them. Each of his films show a love of learning, of pushing back the boundaries. Cruise: "Suddenly, he'll say something to you, or you'll see how he creates a shot, and you realise this man is different, this man is profound. And it seems without effort. You come out of this experience and realise the possibilities of film, the possibilities of how to communicate ideas and concepts in a way that you never thought."

Kubrick wanted to reshoot Leigh's scene with Cruise. However, by this time, Leigh had already started in the lead role of David Cronenberg's *eXistenZ*, so she was replaced by Swedish actress Marie Richardson (*The Best Intentions*). Tom Cruise flew back to England to redo his scene with Richardson in April and May 1998. Principle photography ended in June 1998. Filming eventually stretched to 18 months and the budget went up to $60 million. For all the flak Kubrick got for being slow, that's pretty cheap for a Tom Cruise movie.

On 2 March 1999, Cruise and Kidman, as well as Warner Brothers chairmen Terry Semel and Robert Daly saw the final cut in New York which ran to 2 hours and 19 minutes. Everybody was happy with it. Except for adding the titles and some fine tuning of sound and colour quality, *Eyes Wide Shut* was complete.

On 6 March 1999, Terry Semel talked with Kubrick concerning the marketing campaign and small additions to the score, which is mostly classical music. Kubrick was very excited by the positive response to the screening, and told Julian Senior, his closest colleague at Warner Brothers' London office, *Eyes Wide Shut* was, "my best film ever."

On Sunday, 7 March 1999, Kubrick died in his sleep from a massive heart attack. He was 70, was one of the world's most respected directors and received numerous tributes.

The sexual nature of the film bothered the film business community. Explicit sex in major American film means a NC-17 rating and no money at the box office, even with Tom Cruise and Nicole Kidman fronting it. To avoid the NC-17 rating in America the orgy scene was partially censored with the placement of computer-generated objects and characters in front of the more sexually explicit details. The European theatrical release remains uncut.

The Verdict: This is the work of a mature artist who is still probing the human psyche to find out how it works. Kubrick finds that men are set in their ways, blinkered, patronising, misogynistic. Men try to mask their feelings but, in this case, Bill starts to realise that he does not possess his wife, he cannot control her thoughts and dreams. He takes off his mask (Alice helps take it off - it is in bed with them) and they agree to start again. Beautiful. 5/5

Reference Materials

Books

Stanley Kubrick by Vincent LoBrutto, UK: Faber & Faber, 1998, Paperback, 589 pages, £14.99, ISBN 0571193935, US: Da Capo Press, 1999, Paperback, 606 pages, $17.95, ISBN 0306809060. The best of the Kubrick biographies. LoBrutto has interviewed friends, family and colleagues, has done his research and has found that there is very little to find. Workmanlike, he takes us through the films and the people involved, giving very little insight into the subtext of the films, but explaining how the films were financed, written, filmed and received by the critics. He pays close attention to the technical innovations - perhaps we hear a little too much about focal lengths and lens. It tells you how Kubrick got to be respected in the film-making community.

The Cinema Of Stanley Kubrick by Norman Kagan, UK: Roundhouse Publishing, 1997, Paperback, 264 pages, £10.99, ISBN 1857100263, US: Continuum, 1997, Paperback, 264 pages, $18.95, ISBN 0826404227. There is much to like in this film-by-film analysis but, equally, there are errors which I hope are corrected in the latest edition. Kagan rigorously analyses the films in a manner which I haven't seen elsewhere, but then he is sometimes too rigid and tries to make some films fit his preordained view. On the plus side, there are well-chosen quotes from reviews. So, all in all a mixed bag, but a bag worth rooting through for the odd gem here and there. It has been updated to include all the films up to *Eyes Wide Shut*.

Stanley Kubrick Directs by Alexander Walker, Sybil Taylor, Ulrich Ruchti, UK: Weidenfeld, 1999, Hardcover, 368 pages, £25.00, ISBN 0297824031, US: W W Norton, 1999, Hardcover, 368 pages, $35.00, ISBN 039304601X. This is an updated edition of the 1971 original. Walker is very lucid and interesting all the way through - the attraction here is that Walker takes us through the scenes, frame by frame, cut by cut - there are over 350 black and white film stills. So, equally interesting for those who have or haven't seen the films in question. Kubrick gave Walker access and interviews. The book also features interviews with people Kubrick worked with, as well as commentary on his films and the ideas behind them.

Stanley Kubrick by Michel Ciment, Collins, 1983, Paperback, 238 pages. A unique book, made in collaboration with Kubrick, containing three interviews (on *A Clockwork Orange*, *Barry Lyndon* and *The Shining*), plus interviews with some of Kubrick's collaborators. Ciment contributes some perceptive essays and notes. There are great photos, many of which were selected by Kubrick who made frame enlargements from the original film. Highly recommended. An updated edition is due as I go to press.

Stanley Kubrick by John Baxter, UK: HarperCollins, 1998, Paperback, 416 pages, £9.99, ISBN 0006384455, US: Carroll & Graf, Paperback, 384 pages, $13.95, ISBN 0786704853. A biography which presents Kubrick in a bad light.

Perspectives On Stanley Kubrick by Mario Falsetto (Editor), US: G. K. Hall, 1996, Hardcover, $55.00, ISBN 0816119910. A compilation of writings about Kubrick's films covers *Killer's Kiss* to *Full Metal Jacket*, includes an article by Kubrick, and a piece by Anthony Burgess on Kubrick's adaptation of *A Clockwork Orange*.

Eyes Wide Open: A Memoir Of Stanley Kubrick by Frederic Raphael, UK: Orion, 1999, Hardcover, 186 pages, £12.99, ISBN 0752818686, US: Ballantine Books, 1999, Trade Paperback, $12.00, ISBN 0345437764. Frederic Raphael first met Stanley Kubrick in the early 1970s. This is an account of their long conversations as the screenplay of *Eyes Wide Shut* was written. Raphael's ego seems bruised by the encounters and consequently the book appears to be spiteful.

The Making Of Kubrick's 2001 by Jerome Agel, Signet, 1970, Paperback, 368 pages. If you ever find this, pick it up and just delve straight in. It contains a 96-page photo insert retelling the *2001* story with comments/notes, interviews with everybody. It reprints news, articles, reviews, includes Kubrick's *Playboy* interview. You must have it.

The Lost Worlds Of 2001 by Arthur C Clarke, Sidgwick And Jackson, 1974, Paperback, 240 pages. This time we hear about *2001* from Arthur C Clarke's point of view. Unlike other books, which try to unlock the enigma of a man called Kubrick, Clarke treats Kubrick as a fellow traveller on the road to discovery. Clarke's measured tone and erudite discourse will make you think about the meaning of the film.

2001: Filming The Future by Piers Bizony, Aurum Press, 2000, Paperback, £14.95, ISBN 1854107062. An all-singing, all-dancing making of *2001*. Every aspect of the creation of the film is discussed with colour photos from the filming, preparatory drawings, the MacCall advertising paintings and many revealing anecdotes about working with Kubrick.

Screening The Novel: Rediscovered American Fiction In Film by Gabriel Miller, Frederick Ungar, Paperback, 208 pages, $6.95, ISBN 0804465045. Interesting for its analysis of both book and film of *Paths Of Glory*.

Websites

The Kubrick Site - http://www.alta.demon.co.uk/amk/ - http://amk.atc.dmacc.cc.ia.us - Well, this is THE Kubrick site. A non-profit resource archive for documentary materials maintained by the alt.movies.kubrick newsgroup and its participants. It contains Essays & Articles, Debate & Discussion, Reviews & Press Materials, Scripts & Transcripts, Interviews & Depositions. There are 7, yes SEVEN, interviews with Kubrick, and contributions from Michel Ciment, Penelope Gilliatt, Joseph Gelmis, Samuel R Delany, Lester Del Rey, Barry Norman and Pauline Kael. Since most editions of Anthony Burgess' novel *A Clockwork Orange* only have 20 chapters, the 21st is presented here. And for those wondering what the source story for *AI* was, there's 'Super-Toys Last All Summer Long' by Brian Aldiss. Simply the best site about Kubrick you will ever find.

The Unofficial Eyes Wide Shut Site - http://www.uni-mainz.de/~ruscc000/eyeswideshut - Obviously you can go to the official site which has multimedia stuff, but sometimes it's just more fun going to another place. This site fills in a lot of background about all the rumours and news items that appeared during the making of *Eyes Wide Shut*, and also has a useful links page, where you can get to other decent sites - one is actually hunting down and scanning in copies of *Look* magazine with Kubrick's photos.

The Essential Library: Best-Sellers

Build up your library with new titles every month

Alfred Hitchcock by Paul Duncan, £3.99

More than 20 years after his death, Alfred Hitchcock is still a household name, most people in the Western world have seen at least one of his films, and he popularised the action movie format we see every week on the cinema screen. He was both a great artist and dynamite at the box office. This book examines the genius and enduring popularity of one of the most influential figures in the history of the cinema!

Orson Welles by Martin Fitzgerald

The popular myth is that after the artistic success of *Citizen Kane* it all went downhill for Orson Welles, that he was some kind of fallen genius. Yet, despite overwhelming odds, he went on to make great Films Noirs like *The Lady From Shanghai* and *Touch Of Evil*. He translated Shakespeare's work into films with heart and soul (*Othello*, *Chimes At Midnight*, *Macbeth*), and he gave voice to bitterness, regret and desperation in *The Magnificent Ambersons* and *The Trial*. Far from being down and out, Welles became one of the first cutting-edge independent film-makers.

Woody Allen (Revised & Updated Edition) by Martin Fitzgerald, £3.99

Woody Allen: Neurotic. Jewish. Funny. Inept. Loser. A man with problems. Or so you would think from the characters he plays in his movies. But hold on. Allen has written and directed 30 films. He may be a funny man, but he is also one of the most serious American film-makers of his generation. This revised and updated edition includes *Sweet And Lowdown* and *Small Time Crooks*.

Film Noir by Paul Duncan, £3.99

The laconic private eye, the corrupt cop, the heist that goes wrong, the femme fatale with the rich husband and the dim lover - these are the trademark characters of Film Noir. This book charts the progression of the Noir style as a vehicle for film-makers who wanted to record the darkness at the heart of American society as it emerged from World War to the Cold War. As well as an introduction explaining the origins of Film Noir, seven films are examined in detail and an exhaustive list of over 500 Films Noirs are listed.

Noir Fiction by Paul Duncan, £3.99

For every light that shines, there must always fall a shadow, a dark side - Noir. Noir has infiltrated our world, like some insidious disease, and we cannot get rid of it. The threads of its growth and development have been hinted at but no-one has yet tried to bind them together, to weave the whole picture. This book takes you down the dark highways of the Noir experience, and examines the history of Noir in literature, art, film, and pulps. Sensitive readers are warned - you may find the Noir world disturbing, terrifying and ultimately pessimistic. Features: Jim Thompson, Cornell Woolrich, David Goodis, James Ellroy, Derek Raymond, Charles Willeford and more.

The Essential Library: Recent Releases

Build up your library with new titles every month

Tim Burton by Colin Odell & Michelle Le Blanc, £3.99

Tim Burton makes films about outsiders on the periphery of society. His heroes are psychologically scarred, perpetually naive and childlike, misunderstood or unintentionally disruptive. They upset convential society and morality. Even his villains are rarely without merit - circumstance blurs the divide between moral fortitude and personal action. But most of all, his films have an aura of the fairytale, the fantastical and the magical.

French New Wave by Chris Wiegand, £3.99

The directors of the French New Wave were the original film geeks - a collection of celluloid-crazed cinéphiles with a background in film criticism and a love for American auteurs. Having spent countless hours slumped in Parisian cinémathèques, they armed themselves with handheld cameras, rejected conventions, and successfully moved movies out of the studios and on to the streets at the end of the 1950s.

Borrowing liberally from the varied traditions of film noir, musicals and science fiction, they released a string of innovative and influential pictures, including the classics *Jules Et Jim* and *A Bout De Souffle*. By the mid-1960s, the likes of Jean-Luc Godard, François Truffaut, Claude Chabrol, Louis Malle, Eric Rohmer and Alain Resnais had changed the rules of film-making forever.

Bollywood by Ashok Banker, £3.99

Bombay's prolific Hindi-language film industry is more than just a giant entertainment juggernaut for 1 billion-plus Indians worldwide. It's a part of Indian culture, language, fashion and lifestyle. It's also a great bundle of contradictions and contrasts, like India itself. Thrillers, horror, murder mysteries, courtroom dramas, Hong Kong-style action gunfests, romantic comedies, soap operas, mythological costume dramas... they're all blended with surprising skill into the musical boy-meets-girl formula of Bollywood. This vivid introduction to Bollywood, written by a Bollywood scriptwriter and media commentator, examines 50 major films in entertaining and intimate detail.

Mike Hodges by Mark Adams, £3.99

Features an extensive interview with Mike Hodges. His first film, *Get Carter*, has achieved cult status (recently voted the best British film ever in *Hotdog* magazine) and continues to be the benchmark by which every British crime film is measured. His latest film, *Croupier*, was such a hit in the US that is was re-issued in the UK. His work includes crime drama (*Pulp*), science-fiction (*Flash Gordon* and *The Terminal Man*), comedy (*Morons From Outer Space*) and watchable oddities such as *A Prayer For The Dying* and *Black Rainbow*. Mike Hodges is one of the great maverick British filmmakers.

The Essential Library: Currently Available

Film Directors:

Woody Allen (Revised)	Tim Burton	Ang Lee
Jane Campion*	John Carpenter	Steve Soderbergh
Jackie Chan	Joel & Ethan Coen	Clint Eastwood
David Cronenberg	Terry Gilliam*	Michael Mann
Alfred Hitchcock	Krzysztof Kieslowski*	
Stanley Kubrick	Sergio Leone	
David Lynch	Brian De Palma*	
Sam Peckinpah*	Ridley Scott	
Orson Welles	Billy Wilder	
Steven Spielberg	Mike Hodges	

Film Genres:

Blaxploitation Films	Bollywood	French New Wave
Horror Films	Slasher Movies	Spaghetti Westerns
Vampire Films*	Film Noir	Heroic Bloodshed*

Film Subjects:

Laurel & Hardy	Marx Brothers	Animation
Steve McQueen*	Marilyn Monroe	The Oscars®
Filming On A Microbudget	Bruce Lee	Film Music

TV:

Doctor Who

Literature:

Cyberpunk	Philip K Dick	The Beat Generation
Agatha Christie	Sherlock Holmes	Noir Fiction*
Terry Pratchett	Hitchhiker's Guide	Alan Moore

Ideas:

Conspiracy Theories	Nietzsche	UFOs
Feminism	Freud & Psychoanalysis	

History:

Alchemy & Alchemists	The Crusades	The Black Death
Jack The Ripper	The Rise Of New Labour	Ancient Greece
American Civil War	American Indian Wars	

Miscellaneous:

The Madchester Scene	Stock Market Essentials
How To Succeed As A Sports Agent	

Available at all good bookstores or send a cheque (payable to 'Oldcastle Books') to: **Pocket Essentials (Dept SK2), 18 Coleswood Rd, Harpenden, Herts, AL5 1EQ, UK**. £3.99 each (£2.99 if marked with an *) . For each book add 50p postage & packing in the UK and £1 elsewhere.